Concealed Carry and Self-Defense: Technical and Legal Considerations—

A Case for Universal Reciprocity

Frank T. Traceski

ISBN 10: 1523792302
ISBN 13: 978-1523792306
Library of Congress Control Number: 2016904567
CreateSpace Independent Publishing Platform, North
Charleston, SC

This book is dedicated to my uncle Anthony J. Krejmas, who served as a platoon sergeant in the US 5th Marine Division at Iwo Jima during World War II. After the war he also served on a Second Amendment task force aimed at preserving the right to bear arms.

CONTENTS

3. Types of Ammunition   33

4. Ammunition Evaluation   45

5. Criminal Law   69

List of Tables

Preface

A man from Maine was arrested after being pulled over in Massachusetts for operating a motor vehicle under the influence. He was carrying a handgun concealed in his car. When asked by the arresting police officer if he had a license for the gun, the man replied, "I only need the Second Amendment."

If you are naïve enough to believe this man was right, then you most certainly need to read this book. That answer might have been acceptable for carrying a firearm while riding a horse through the countryside more than two hundred years ago, but it's not acceptable today.

If you are not a criminal with criminal intent and you carry a concealed handgun, you probably intend it as an insurance policy against a life-threatening situation that you hope will never occur. Your purpose is to be prepared to defend yourself or others in such a situation. Today, to carry a concealed handgun legally, you must have an appropriate concealed-carry license in almost every state.

If you don't have a license, you may face serious criminal charges and possibly prison time. Getting a license to carry a concealed firearm is a complicated, time-consuming, and expensive process. Even with a handgun permit, there are restrictions on where you can carry a concealed handgun. This book is intended to make the reader aware of current restrictions on concealed carry and the laws of self-defense.

Origin of this Book

I first thought about writing this book after taking several concealed-carry and firearm-safety courses required for obtaining handgun permits. During the courses, the instructors did not adequately address many technical and legal questions. Afterward, I began a lengthy process of personal research to answer my own questions about concealed carry and self-defense.

I wrote this book to fill in a gap I have not seen covered adequately in many other books. Not every concealed-carry holder is a criminal lawyer, and yet, given the complexities of today's gun laws, one has to be as smart and knowledgeable as a lawyer to stay out of trouble. This book is intended to call attention to the legal dangers not easily anticipated or avoided when carrying a concealed handgun. Driving state to state with a concealed handgun is a good example.

Purpose of this Book

This book is primarily intended for individuals who are licensed to carry a concealed handgun or are taking a course to get certified for concealed carry; firearms instructors who are teaching certification courses for concealed carry or handgun safety; practicing criminal lawyers (prosecutors and defense attorneys); and the general public. Its purpose is to educate and inform those who have the need or desire to understand the fundamental technical and legal concepts associated with concealed carry of a handgun and the justifiable use of that handgun in self-defense.

The matter of self-defense with a handgun is very complicated. There have been many recent criminal trials of homeowners who shot and killed people, either inside or just outside their homes, and claimed self-defense. In many of these cases, the shooter has been convicted of murder instead of being found innocent under the claim of self-defense. Many of these convicted individuals were obviously not aware of the legal principles of self-defense.

Learning about these principles after a shooting is not a good option. If you carry a concealed handgun, knowing under what circumstances you are justified in using deadly force with a handgun is essential. This book will inform the reader of current laws and principles of self-defense with a handgun.

Content of this Book

Chapters 1 through 4 cover the technical considerations contained in this book. Chapter 1 addresses concealed carry in the US and why more people may be choosing to do so, and assesses an FBI report on active shootings in the US. Chapters 2 and 3 describe the most common types of handguns and ammunition that are used for concealed carry and self-defense. The topic of ammunition evaluation, its history and methodology are discussed in Chapter 4. Chapters 5-10 discuss various legal considerations, including criminal law, concealed carry restrictions, self-defense laws, and related federal and state firearms laws.

The material discussed in this book is intended only as a concise summary and a top-level overview of the subjects addressed. Therefore, I suggest a variety of other books and sources that go into much more detail on these subjects. The sources I recommend are based on my personal experience and research on the subject matter.

Inherent in any discussion of firearms laws is the issue of gun control. I acknowledge my belief up front that more gun control laws are not the answer to reducing gun violence in the United States. The latter part of this book addresses gun control trends and politics. Whatever your view is on gun control, Chapters 9 and 10 provide some food for thought.

A Case for Universal Reciprocity

Many federal and state gun laws are ambiguous and sometimes contradictory. Some laws are not based in common sense, and others are outright absurd. Many laws actually make it virtually impossible for an individual to exercise his or her right to self-defense. Driving from state to state with a concealed handgun is one example.

One solution is to pass a federal law for "universal" reciprocity for concealed carry. With universal concealed carry a person authorized to carry a concealed handgun issued by one of the states will be legally authorized to carry in each of the other forty-nine states. A new federal law, such as a Constitutional Concealed Carry Reciprocity Act, passed by the US Congress, could accomplish this goal. Such a law would make it easier, less expensive, and more user friendly to carry concealed handguns for self-defense in all fifty states.

Furthermore, there are many locations where concealed carry of firearms is currently prohibited but should be allowed. Active shootings are occurring with increasing frequency throughout the country and armed citizens may be able to reduce the body counts. In Chapter 10, I propose some legislative changes to gun laws.

I hope readers will find this book interesting, informative, and educational.

Frank T. Traceski
April 15, 2016

Disclaimer

Knowledge of gun laws is an important first step in becoming a responsible gun owner. The legal concepts discussed herein merely serve as a starting point for the reader. It is incumbent upon all gun owners to know all the relevant federal, state, and local laws that apply to their situations. They must also know how to safely handle and operate their firearms.

The author takes no responsibility as to the accuracy of laws discussed or for the validity of the technical data taken from outside sources. Gun laws are continuously changing, and the circumstances of any given situation determine the ultimate legality and disposition. The examples of state and federal gun laws cited in this book are merely intended to introduce the reader to the legal concepts involved.

This publication provides the author's beliefs and opinions in regard to the subject matter covered. This book is sold with the understanding that neither the author nor the publisher is providing professional, legal, firearm instruction, or other services through the dissemination of this publication.

Finally, the author is not an attorney, and this book does not offer legal advice. If you are in need of legal advice, consult a competent attorney in your jurisdiction.

Chapter 1

Introduction

And that the Constitution shall never be construed to authorize Congress to prevent the people of the United States from keeping their own arms.
—Samuel Adams, debates of the Massachusetts Convention of 1788

This book's primary scope is concerned with those legal considerations that apply to the concealed carry of handguns for self-defense purposes. Every citizen in the United States who is licensed to carry a handgun must be aware of the fundamental laws and legal restrictions imposed upon him or her in modern times. Being unaware of the law might result in violations that then lead to misdemeanor or felony charges and convictions that carry heavy fines or even prison time.

In addition to understanding all applicable gun laws, any US citizen who obtains a license to carry must have a thorough understanding of the handguns and ammunition used for self-defense purposes. Therefore, chapters relating to the basic types of handguns and ammunition in common usage, ammunition evaluation, and handgun terminology are included.

Throughout this book, real-life examples are provided of mistakes people have made or crimes people have committed while carrying concealed handguns. Other events also serve to illustrate what to be aware of and what not to do.

Chapter 1 defines concealed carry, discusses why someone might want to carry a concealed handgun for self-defense where permissible, and reveals the approximate number of concealed-carry holders in the United States. The suggested reading sources cited provide detail about how to carry concealed handguns.

What Is Concealed Carry?

"Concealed carry" refers to the practice of carrying a handgun in public outside of ordinary view, either on one's person or in close proximity to one's person. It is also frequently referred to as carrying a concealed weapon (CCW). This term might apply to a loaded handgun located in the glove compartment or under a seat in a car or in a briefcase or purse. In any of those cases, the gun is not in plain view, and it is readily accessible.

Suggested reading:

Ayoob, Massad. *Gun Digest Book of Concealed Carry*. 2nd ed. Iola, Wisconsin: Krause, 2012.

Fitzpatrick, Brad. *Shooter's Bible Guide to Concealed Carry*. New York: Skyhorse, 2013.

Why Carry a Concealed Handgun?

Whether to carry a concealed handgun for personal protection is an individual choice based on a number of factors and personal beliefs. One important factor that cannot escape one's attention is that in today's society, mass shootings and other firearms killings seem to occur just about everywhere and are occurring with increasing frequency.

The FBI published a report in 2014 on active shooter incidents in the United States between 2000 and 2013. The FBI study examined 160 active shooting incidents. A detailed tally of the incidents and the findings are documented in the FBI report cited below. One conclusion is particularly evident. Active shootings are on the rise.

This trend reinforces the need to focus on law enforcement's prevention efforts as well as armed citizens carrying concealed weapons. After all, these people might be able to respond to active shootings more quickly than the police. Whereas police response time is measured in minutes, a trained and armed citizen carrying a concealed weapon can typically respond in seconds.

Every day in the United States, there are armed robberies in convenience stores, banks, and gas stations. There are drug arrests accompanied by illegal gun possession. It doesn't seem safe anywhere anymore. In fact, in 2010 a Massachusetts man murdered four family members, and that included slashing the throats of his two young children. He spent a night on the run just two miles down the road from my home.

Why carry a concealed firearm? The simple answer is to be prepared for a life-threatening situation with the hope that a firearm might be able to save your life or the lives of other threatened people. Concealed carry is an insurance policy against the criminals and disturbed people who walk around us everywhere. You never know when a legally carried concealed handgun might save your life.

FBI Study of Active Shootings

The FBI conducted a study of active shooting incidents to provide federal, state, and local law enforcement officials with data so they could better understand how to prevent, prepare for, respond to, and recover from these incidents. In the study, the FBI identified 160 active shooting incidents that occurred in the United States between 2000 and 2013 (Blair and Schweit 2014).

The report identified an active shooter as an "individual actively engaged in killing or attempting to kill people in a confined and populated area." The study included the high-casualty shootings at Virginia Tech (2007); Fort Hood (2009); Aurora, Colorado (2012); Sandy Hook (2012); and the Washington Navy Yard (2012). Since this study, the Umpqua Community College shooting in Roseburg, Oregon, and the San Bernardino shooting occurred in 2015.

What I find particularly enlightening about this study are its findings concerning (1) the nature of active shootings, (2) the locations of the shootings, (3) the short time intervals of the incidents during which maximum damage occurred, and (4) the final resolution or outcomes regarding the shooter(s). All four factors have implications for the concealed carry of handguns. My comments noted below in brackets are not part of the FBI report.

(1) Nature of the shootings. The term *active shooter* is used by law enforcement to describe a situation in which a shooting is in progress. The "active" aspect of the crime inherently implies that both law enforcement personnel and citizens have the potential to affect the outcome of the event based upon their responses. [A citizen carrying a concealed handgun falls into this category.]

(2) Locations of the shootings. Nearly half (45.6 percent) of the shootings occurred in areas of commerce, including businesses both open and closed to pedestrian traffic. The second-largest location grouping was educational environments (24.4 percent), where for the most part carrying concealed is prohibited. Other locations included government properties (10 percent), residences (4.4 percent), houses of worship (3.8 percent), and health care facilities (2.5 percent). The majority of the shootings occurred in areas of commerce [where armed citizens who are legally carrying concealed could potentially be factors in stopping active shooters].

(3) Short time intervals of the shootings. The lethal carnage and serious wounds inflicted by the shooters occurred in a matter of minutes. Of 64 incidents where the duration of the incident was ascertained, 44 (69.0 percent) ended in five minutes or less, with 23 ending in two minutes or less. There is very little time for law enforcement to respond, and in fact, in only 45 (28.1 percent) of the 160 incidents, law enforcement and the shooter exchanged gunfire. [An armed citizen carrying a concealed handgun at the shooting location while it is occurring is in a much better position to stop the shooter(s) and save lives than law enforcement who arrive much later, —after most of the shooting is already done. The same can be said about armed guards on location.]

(4) Final outcomes of the shootings. Of the 160 incidents, 90 (56.3 percent) ended on the shooter's initiative. In some cases the shooter committed suicide or just stopped shooting. Other times the shooter fled the scene. Sixty percent of the incidents ended before police arrived. [Again, an armed citizen or armed guard might be able to stop the shooter before law enforcement arrives.]

The FBI report also cites five incidents (3.1 percent) where the shootings ended after armed individuals who were not law enforcement personnel exchanged gunfire with the shooters. This low percentage of shootings ended by armed citizens might not seem like much. However, this number might be directly related to the fact that less than 5 percent of the general population have concealed-carry permits, and, even with permits, those people are prohibited from concealed carry of firearms in many locations.

Current laws prohibit carrying handguns (even with a permit) in most schools and federal buildings. That includes military bases and post offices. Some states are starting to certify teachers who are willing to carry concealed handguns in some schools.

Number of Concealed-Carry Permits

According to the US General Accountability Office (GAO), there were approximately eight million active permits to carry concealed handguns in the United States as of December 31, 2011. States and local authorities control the issuance of concealed-carry permits. There is currently no federal law specifically addressing the issuance of concealed-carry permits at the state level (GAO 2012).

In recent years, the total number of concealed-carry handgun permits in the United States has increased substantially. Data collected by the Crime Prevention Research Center (CPRC) shows there were 11,113,013 Americans (approximately 4.8 percent of the total population) in 2014 who had concealed-carry permits.

Table 1. Number of Concealed-Carry Permits in the US

Year	Number of Permits
1999	2.7 million
2007	4.6 million
2011	8.0 million
2014	11.1 million

Source: (US GAO 2012, Whitley 2014)

The number of permits issued (as determined in this study) does not represent the true figure of Americans who are legally carrying concealed firearms. There are three reasons for this. Six states do not require a license for concealed carry; data for the study was not readily available from all states; and for some states, the data was old and did not capture the recent growth in the number of permits issued (Whitley 2014).

What Is Self-Defense?

Self-defense is the use of force to protect oneself or one's family from a real or threatened attack. Generally, a person is justified in using deadly force in self-defense or in defense of another only if defending against another's deadly force or threat of serious bodily harm.

Suggested reading:

Branca, Andrew F. 2013. *The Law of Self-Defense*: *The Indispensable Guide for the Armed Citizen*. Maynard, Massachusetts: Law of Self-Defense.

Vilos, Mitch, and Evan Vilos. 2010. *Self-Defense Laws of All 50 States*. Centerville, Utah: Guns West.

In the next chapter, we look at what types of handguns are used for personal protection and where to get more specific information.

Chapter 2

Types of Handguns

Get rid of that nickel-plated sissy pistol and get yourself a Glock.
Tommy Lee Jones to Robert Downey Jr., *US Marshals* (1998)

The terms *handgun* and *pistol* are used synonymously throughout this book. By definition, a pistol or handgun is a firearm that has a short barrel and is designed to be held, aimed, and fired with one hand. Although the term *pistol* is used frequently to refer to semiautomatic handguns, it is still proper to use the word *pistol* to refer to all types of handguns. This chapter deals primarily with the two most common types of handguns in use today for concealed carry: the revolver and the semiautomatic handgun.

Suggested reading:

Hartnik, A. E. 2002. *The Complete Encyclopedia of Pistols and Revolvers.* Edison, New Jersey: Chartwell Books.

Chapter 2 describes the basic types and mechanics of revolvers and semiautomatic pistols and what to consider in selecting a handgun for self-defense; identifies some specific types of handguns by well-known manufacturers; and provides reasons why an individual may be prohibited from purchasing a handgun. Some suggested reading sources are cited that provide extensive information on handguns. However, individual company product catalogs or websites are the best places to learn detailed information on their handguns. Catalogs provide nice colored pictures that can be carried around to show and discuss with other people.

Revolvers

A revolver is a type of handgun that has a rotating (or revolving) cylinder containing a number of firing chambers. The action of the trigger or hammer will line up a chamber with the barrel and firing pin.

Revolvers may generally be classified as either single action or double action. In single-action revolvers, the trigger performs only one function: releasing the hammer to fire the pistol. In double-action revolvers, the trigger performs two functions: it cocks and releases the hammer, firing the handgun. Most double-action revolvers may also be fired in single-action mode by manually cocking the hammer with the thumb.

Single action only (SA). The hammer of single-action revolvers must be manually cocked by the shooter, typically using a thumb, for each shot. The trigger performs only one action, releasing the hammer. Examples of single-action revolvers are the Smith & Wesson Schofield .45, first produced in 1875 and used by Jesse James; the Army Colt .45 Classic Peacemaker; and the Navy Colt .36 revolver, which was discontinued in 1873.

Double action/single action (DA/SA). Pulling the trigger of double-action revolvers will cock and release the hammer. The trigger performs two actions. Most double-action revolvers may also be shot by cocking the hammer manually (i.e., single-action mode). Hence, the designation DA/SA is used because these revolvers may be fired two different ways. Examples of DA/SA revolvers are the Ruger GP141 and S&W Model 617.

Double action only (DAO). These types of revolvers may only be fired in double-action mode, whereby the trigger cocks and releases the hammer. Pulling the hammer back to fire in single action is not possible. A S&W Model 642 Airweight revolver is an example of a DAO type revolver.

Semiautomatic Handguns (Autoloaders)

A semiautomatic handgun, also frequently called an autoloader, is a self-loading firearm that reloads itself after each shot. This type of handgun generally contains cartridges in a magazine located in the grip of the handgun. When an autoloading handgun is fired, the spent cartridge that contained the bullet and propellant is ejected, the firing mechanism is cocked, and a new cartridge is chambered. Semiautomatic handguns require the trigger to be pulled each time in order to fire a round.

Semiautomatic or self-loading pistols may be classified into the following three categories based upon their trigger action:

Single action only (SA). Single-action self-loading handguns are usually carried with a round in the chamber, the hammer cocked, and with the manual safety in the "on" position. This condition is called "cocked and locked." Pulling the trigger performs only one function, releasing the hammer. The Colt Model 1911 is an example of a single-action semiautomatic (autoloader).

Double-action/single-action (DA/SA). In this type of self-loader, the first shot is fired in double-action mode with a longer, heavier trigger pull to both cock and release the hammer (two functions). All subsequent shots are fired in single-action mode. The movement of the slide will cock the hammer or internal firing mechanism for all successive shots. The trigger only performs one function, releasing the hammer or internal firing mechanism. These types of handguns are frequently just called double-action semiautomatics.

An example of this type is the Walther PPK/S. A warning advisory in its instruction manual warns the shooter, "The single-action trigger pull is much lighter and shorter than the double-action pull. Before you put your finger on the trigger, be sure you look at the trigger or hammer to see if you are in single or double action."

Double action only (DAO). In this type of semiauto, the trigger will cock and release the hammer or internal firing mechanism on all shots, first and subsequent shots. The trigger performs two actions. The slide will chamber a cartridge after each shot, but it will not cock the hammer. A DAO semiauto handgun has the same trigger pull length and weight each time.

Handguns such as Glock pistols use a firing pin (also called a striker) and are hammerless. Glocks act like DAO semi-autos since they have the same trigger pull length and weight each time (about 5.5 pounds).

Handgun Choices for Self-Defense

For those who decide to have a handgun for self-defense (either in the home or for concealed carry), a choice must be made as to what type and caliber of handgun and ammunition to use. A primary consideration is whether to select a revolver or a semiautomatic (autoloader) handgun. Both types have advantages and disadvantages, and again it is up to the user to make a personal and informed choice.

Revolvers and Semiauto Pistols

Revolver advantages:
• safer and easier to handle for inexperienced shooters
• a misfire does not put the gun out of action
• better overall reliability, doesn't jam as easily
Revolver disadvantages:
• more bulky

• much slower to load
• less comfortable to conceal on your person
Semiauto pistol advantages:
• more compact, easier and faster to load and clean
• easier and more comfortable to conceal
• ammunition capacity is larger
Semiauto pistol disadvantages:
• jamming and misfires can disable the weapon
• more dangerous to handle

Suggested reading:

Bird, Chris. 2004. "Choosing a Handgun: Semiautomatics and Revolvers." Chapter 5 in *The Concealed Handgun Manual: How to Choose, Carry, and Shoot a Gun in Self-Defense.* San Antonio, Texas: Privateer Publications.

There are many excellent books and magazines that cover the topic of selecting a handgun for self-defense. The books by Massad Ayoob and Brad Fitzpatrick suggested in chapter 1 are excellent choices. The United States Concealed Carry Association (USCCA) publishes the monthly *Concealed Carry Magazine.* USCCA website www.usconcealedcarry.com.

Suggested reading:

Fitzpatrick, Brad. 2013. "Choosing a Firearm for Concealed Carry." Chapter 8 in *Shooter's Bible Guide to Concealed Carry.* New York: Skyhorse.

The *Gun Digest* is an excellent annual reference book of the various types of handguns that are available in the commercial marketplace. *Gun Digest 2013* lists 348 manufacturers and importers along with their websites.

Suggested reading:

Lee, Jerry, ed. 2014. *Gun Digest 2015*, 69th ed. Iola, Wisconsin: Krause.

Considering "Stopping Power"

In choosing a handgun, one must also consider the caliber of the handgun, its ammunition, and its "stopping power." In a self-defense situation, the purpose of a handgun is to instantly incapacitate the aggressor(s). According to Dr. W. French Anderson's forensic analysis of the Miami FBI shootout of 1986 (discussed in more detail in chapter 4), the most effective way to incapacitate an aggressor is to stop their brain or heart from functioning.

The most effective caliber of ammunition for this purpose has been the subject of much study and debate over many decades, and some disagreement still remains among various experts. Ultimately, the caliber of handgun to use is a personal choice after considering many factors.

Historically, one gray or uncertain area in stopping power concerns 9 mm- and .38-Special cartridges. Below these calibers (e.g., .22 LR, .25 ACP, .32 ACP, .380 ACP) the handguns are generally smaller and more concealable, but have less energy for penetration and are not considered as effective as the higher calibers (see Appendix A for definition of caliber acronyms and chapter 4 for a more detailed discussion of stopping power). After the Miami FBI shootout, it was determined that .38+P Special and 9 mm cartridges were not powerful enough for instant incapacitation. Subsequently, the FBI moved up to the 10 mm, and then to the .40 Smith & Wesson (S&W)-caliber where much of law enforcement is today.

Many experts support the view that larger, more powerful calibers are the best choice, up to a limit. Some believe that any good self-defense caliber should start with the number 4, such as .40 S&W and above (e.g., .45 ACP). Nine-millimeter advocates point out ballistic gelatin tests that show smaller, fast bullets are better than bigger, slow bullets. The controversy continues. But you the reader must decide for yourself.

It gets more complicated when you consider the Taylor and Hatcher mathematical formulas and other stopping-power indexes (see chapter 4). More powerful cartridges such as .44 Magnum and above are impractical for most people because of the size of the handgun, the discomfort of carrying it on your person regularly, and its concealability. Powerful cartridges also produce more recoil and muzzle flash and are overpenetrating.

Concealability and Weight

I have already stated briefly some of the advantages and disadvantages of revolvers and semiauto pistols and have provided a general discussion on the importance of stopping power. Two very important considerations for concealed carry of a handgun are the concealability and the weight of the gun.

In 2014 the *Washington Times* posted on its website a list of what it considers the "Best Concealed Carry Handguns for Self-Defense." In total there were fifteen handguns on the list. The handgun manufacturers included Beretta, Colt, Glock, Kahr, Kimber, Ruger, Smith & Wesson, Taurus, and Walther.

Of the fifteen handguns, three were revolvers and twelve were semiauto pistols. All of these handguns were very small in size and very lightweight (typically, twenty ounces or less). It is evident that small size and light weight were the two primary criteria considered for this list.

However, in addition to size and weight, the caliber of a self-defense handgun is a primary consideration, as you will see in more detail in chapter 4. The fifteen handguns on the *Washington Times* list included the following calibers: one .38 Special, five .380 auto, six 9 mm, two .357 Magnum, and one .45 ACP.

The calibers .380 auto and 9 mm dominated the list. As you will see later, these calibers are generally not the "best" in terms of stopping power and muzzle energy. It is evident that the advantages you gain in concealability and light weight may be offset by the reduction in stopping power compared to larger calibers.

Selected Handgun Manufacturers

Ten popular manufacturers of handguns are briefly described in this section in alphabetical order. For each manufacturer I have included a brief history and a list of selected handguns in different calibers that are representative of those useful for concealed carry. For a more detailed look at the manufacturers' handguns, I recommend visiting their websites or obtaining a copy of their most recent catalog of firearms.

Colt

Colt Manufacturing Company LLC
PO Box 1868
Hartford, CT 06144
(800) 962-2658
www.coltsmfg.com

History

Colt Manufacturing Company is a US firearms manufacturer whose predecessor corporation was founded in 1836 by Samuel Colt (1814–62). Samuel Colt got patents for a revolver design from the US government in 1836 based upon percussion-cap technology. Colt designed the .36-caliber Colt Paterson revolver that was used by Texas Rangers (Kyle 2013).

The most famous Colt pistols are the Colt .45 (also known as the Single Action Army, Peacemaker, Model P, or M1873) and the Colt M1911 pistol. The Colt .45 Peacemaker revolver was originally manufactured by Colt from 1873 to 1941. Production of a second generation lasted from 1955 to 1975, and a third generation (1976 to present) continues (Lee 2012).

Colt semiautomatic handgun choices for concealed carry include the Mustang Lite in .380 ACP, the Defender in 9 mm and .45 ACP, and the Combat Commander in 9 mm and .45 ACP. Source: Colt product brochure, 2016

Glock

Glock, Inc.
6000 Highlands Parkway
Smyrna, GA 30082
(770) 432-1202
www.glock.com

History

In the early 1980s Austrian engineer and founder of Glock, Inc. Gaston Glock developed a handgun for the Austrian military to replace its Walther P38 pistol. The Glock 17 handgun was the first to use a polymer frame combined with a steel slide and barrel and it became widely accepted worldwide. For a very interesting history of Glock and his company read, *Glock: The Rise of America's Gun* by Paul M. Barrett.

Glock handguns were introduced into the United States 30 years ago in 1986. The dominance of Glock pistols worldwide in both the civilian and military marketplaces can be attributed to many design and performance advantages. Some of the main advantages are listed in Table 2.

Table 2. Some Advantages of Glock Handguns

Characteristic	Advantage
Low bore axis	Less muzzle flip
Reduced part count (<36)	Better reliability, easy to maintain
Optimized grip angle	Improved pointability
Polymer frame	Durability
Low weight	More comfortable, easier to handle

Source: Kasler, 1992.

Types of Handguns

For a complete guide to Glock pistols, see the *Glock 2016 Buyers Guide*, which can be obtained by calling Glock at 770-432-1202. Some Glock choices for concealed carry and self-defense are listed in Table 3.

Table 3. Selected Glock Handguns

Caliber	Glock Model(s)
9 x 19 mm	G19, G26, G43
10 mm	G29
.40	G23, G27
.357 SIG	G31, G32, G33
.380 ACP	G42
.45 GAP	G37, G38, G39
.45 ACP	G21, G30, G36, G41

Source: *Glock 2016 Buyer's Guide*

Glock handguns are used by over 65 percent of the law enforcement agencies in the US. Glock .40-caliber pistols are the standard of more law enforcement agencies than any other handgun model. Glock pistols in .45 GAP caliber are used by 10 percent of the nation's state police and highway patrol agencies.

Suggested reading:

Barrett, Paul M. 2013. *Glock: The Rise of America's Gun*. New York: Broadway Paperbacks, Random House.

Boatman, Robert H. 2002. *Living with Glocks: The Complete Guide to the New Standard in Combat Handguns*. Boulder, Colorado: Paladin Press.

Kasler, Peter Alan. 1992. *Glock: The New Wave in Combat Handguns*. Boulder, Colorado: Paladin Press.

Long, Duncan. 1996. *Glock's Handguns*. El Dorado, Arkansas: Desert Publications.

PTOOMA Productions. 2004. *The Complete Glock Reference Guide*.

Sweeney, Patrick. 2003. *Glock: A Comprehensive Review (Design, History, Use)*. Iola, Wisconsin: Krause.

Kahr Arms

Kahr Arms, Auto-Ordnance & Magnum Research, Inc.
130 Goddard Memorial Drive
Worcester, MA 01603
(508) 795-3919
www.kahr.com

History

Kahr Arms is an American small-arms manufacturer of compact and midsize semiautomatic pistols in calibers .380 ACP, 9 mm Luger (Parabellum), .40 S&W, and .45 ACP. The company headquarters is currently in Blauvelt, New York, and its manufacturing facility is located in Worcester, Massachusetts. In 2010 Kahr bought Magnum Research, which markets the Desert Eagle handgun.

Table 4. Selected Kahr Arms Handguns

Kahr Model	Caliber(s)
TP Series	9 mm, .40 S&W, .45 ACP
T Series	9 mm, .40 S&W
P Series	.380 ACP, 9 mm, .40 S&W, .45 ACP
PM Series	9 mm, .40 S&W, .45 ACP
K Series	9 mm, .40 S&W
MK Series	9 mm, .40 S&W
CW Series	.380 ACP, 9 mm, .40 S&W, .45 ACP
CM Series	9 mm, .40 S&W, .45ACP

Source: Kahr Arms. *All American*, 2016.

Kimber

Kimber Manufacturing. Inc.
555 Taxter Road, Suite 235
Elmsford, NY 10523
(888) 243-4522
www.kimberamerica.com

History

Kimber Manufacturing is an American manufacturer of small arms and is known primarily for its .45 ACP-caliber M1911 semiautomatic pistols. Originally founded in Oregon in 1979, it now has manufacturing facilities in New York and New Jersey. Kimber has also just introduced a brand-new K6 double-action revolver in caliber .357 Magnum/.38 Special.

Table 5. Selected Kimber Handguns

Semiauto Model(s)	Calibers(s)
Pro Carry II (1911)	9 mm, .45 ACP
Ultra Carry II (1911)	9 mm, .45 ACP
Crimson Carry II (1911)	.45 ACP
Master Carry (1911)	.45 ACP
Super Carry (1911)	.45 ACP
Micro Pistols	.380 ACP, 9 mm
Solo Pistol	9 mm

Source: Kimber. *Lands and Grooves,* 2016.

SIG Sauer

SIG Sauer, Inc.
Global Headquarters
72 Pease Boulevard
Newington, NH 03801
(603) 610-3000
www.sigsauer.com

History

SIG Sauer is one of the largest firearms manufacturing companies in the world. The SIG Sauer line of handguns began in 1975 with the SIG P220. Today SIG Sauer is located in Exeter, New Hampshire, and their world-renowned SIG Sauer Academy is located in Epping, New Hampshire. US Navy SEALS, federal air marshals, and many state and local law enforcements agencies use SIG Sauer handguns.

Table 6. Selected SIG Sauer Handguns

Semiauto Model(s)	Caliber
P290RS	.380 ACP
P225-A1, P226, P229, P239	9 mm
P226, P229, P239	.357 SIG
P226, P229, P239	.40 S&W
P220, P227	.45 ACP

Source: Sig Sauer. *When It Counts*, 2016.

Smith & Wesson

Smith & Wesson
2100 Roosevelt Avenue
Springfield, MA 01104
(800) 331-0852
www.smith-wesson.com

History

Smith & Wesson is a leading manufacturer of firearms founded in 1852 by Horace Smith (1808–1893) and Daniel B. Wesson (1825–1906). In 1856 their new company came out with the Model 1 revolver, which was a .22-caliber seven-shot revolver. Today headquartered in Springfield, Massachusetts, Smith & Wesson manufactures a variety of semiautomatic and revolver handguns and has developed many different ammunition cartridges.

Handguns for Concealed Carry and Self-Defense

Smith & Wesson has such a large variety of revolvers and semiauto pistols, I recommend going to their website directly or getting a copy of their standard catalog.

Suggested reading:

Supica, Jim, and Richard Nahas. 2006. *Standard Catalog of Smith and Wesson*. Iola, Wisconsin: Gun Digest Books.

Springfield Armory

Springfield Armory
420 West Main Street
Genesco, IL 61254
(800) 680-6866
www.springfieldarmory.com

History

The original Springfield Armory located in Springfield, Massachusetts, was created by George Washington in 1777 to store ammunition. The Springfield Armory was a primary US government facility for the manufacture of US military firearms until it was closed in 1968. In 1974 the Springfield Armory name was licensed to the Reese family, who formed the current company. The company in Illinois has no association with the original Springfield Armory, which is a national historic site in Massachusetts.

XD(X-treme Duty) pistols are products licensed and sold by Springfield Armory, Inc., located in Geneseo, Illinois. XD is the marketing name of a series of semi-automatic pistols that are manufactured by a company in Croatia (HS Produkt). The series includes the XD, XDM, and XDS pistols that are noted for their polymer frame.

Table 7. Selected Springfield Armory Handguns

Semiauto Model	Caliber(s)
XDS	.45 ACP
XD Subcompact	9 mm, .40 S&W
XD Compact	.45 ACP
XDM Compact	.45 ACP, 9 mm, .40 S&W

Source: Springfield Armory USA, *2013 Catalog*.

Types of Handguns

Sturm Ruger

Sturm, Ruger & Co., Inc.
Customer Service Department
200 Ruger Road
Prescott, AZ 86301
(336) 949-5200
www.ruger.com

History

The Ruger Company is one of the nation's leading manufacturers of firearms. The company was founded in 1949 in Southport, Connecticut, by William B. Ruger (1916–2002) and Alexander McCormick Sturm (1923–1951). Ruger introduced the highly successful .22-caliber Ruger Standard semiautomatic pistol and manufactures its derivatives, the Ruger MK II and MK III pistols.

Table 8. Selected Ruger Handguns

Type	Model	Caliber(s)
Revolver	LCR	.38 Special +P
Revolver	LCR	.357 Magnum
Revolver	Alaskan	.44 Magnum
Semiauto	LC380	.380 Auto
Semiauto	LCP Compact	.380 Auto
Semiauto	LC9	9 mm
Semiauto	SR Series	9 mm, .40 S&W, .45 ACP

Source: www.ruger.com

Suggested reading:

Wilson, R. L. 2007. *Ruger & His Guns: A History of the Man, the Company, and Their Firearms*. New York: Chartwell Books.

Prasac, Max. 2013. *Gun Digest Book of Ruger Revolvers: The Definitive History.* Iola, Wisconsin: Krause.

Taurus

Taurus Manufacturing
16175 NW 49 Avenue
Miami, FL 33014
(305) 624-1115
www.taurususa.com

History

Taurus is a Brazil-based manufacturing company that began exporting revolvers to the United States in 1968. In 1984 Taurus created a subsidiary, Taurus Manufacturing, to more effectively market handguns in the United States. One of Taurus's most successful semiautomatic handguns is the PT92. Their Raging Bull chambered in .44 Magnum and .454 Casull is a popular hunting handgun.

Table 9. Selected Taurus Handguns

Type	Model	Caliber(s)
Revolver	Taurus-Mini	.380 ACP
Revolver	650/850 CIA	.38 Special, .357 Magnum
Semiauto	Millennium G2	9 mm, .40 S&W
Semiauto	24/7 G2 Compact	.40 S&W, .45 ACP
Semiauto	700 Slim	9 mm, .40 S&W
Semiauto	800 Compact	9 mm, .40 S&W

Source: Taurus. *Carry On*. 2013.

Walther

Walther Arms, Inc.
7700 Chad Colley Boulevard
Fort Smith, AR 72916
(479) 242-8500
www.waltherarms.com

History

The Walther Company goes back to 1886 when gunsmith Carl Walther began making firearms in Germany. Walther manufactures a broad range of firearms, including defense handguns, which are marketed in the United States from a facility in Fort Smith, Arkansas.

Table 10. Selected Walther Handguns

Semiauto Model	Caliber(s)
CCP	9 mm
PPQ M2	9 mm, .40 S&W
PPS M2	9 mm, .40 S&W
P99	9 mm, .40 S&W
PPS Classic	9 mm, .40 S&W
PPK/S	.380 Auto
PK 380	.380 Auto
PPQ 45	.45 ACP

Source: Walther. *Built For Life 2016 Product Catalog.*

Hunting Handguns

Big-bore handguns generally are intended for hunting big game (e.g., bear, elk, moose, and antelope). I do not recommend them for concealed carry unless you are somewhere like Alaska where you might expect to run into a grizzly bear. In addition to being too big to carry concealed comfortably, these guns, by definition, are meant for hunting. If you ever had to claim self-defense at a criminal trial, the prosecuting attorney could make an issue of it. The penetration of hunting handgun cartridges is also much greater, increasing the likelihood of collateral damage, such as killing an innocent bystander who could be hundreds of feet away.

Hunting Handgun Cartridges

Some typical muzzle velocities and energies of selected calibers of hunting handgun cartridges are listed in Table 11.

Table 11. Selected Hunting Handgun Cartridges

Cartridge (caliber)	Weight (grains)	Velocity (ft/sec)	Energy (ft-lb)
.475 Wildey Magnum	250 SP	1,850	1,900
.460 S&W	220 SST	2,200	2,149
.454 Casull	260 JHP	1,723	1,730
.44 Rem Magnum	180 JHP	1,610	1,036

Source: *Cartridges of the World*, 2006.

Charles Bronson's Wildey Magnum in the movie *Death Wish 3* was impressive looking but makes an impractical concealed-carry weapon.

Purchasing a Handgun (Legal Disqualifiers)

An individual wishing to purchase a handgun in a gun store must undergo an instant background check and fill out ATF Form 4473 Purchase of Firearms - Firearms Transaction Record Part I—Over-the-Counter. This form is then used by the seller licensed under 18 U.S.C. § 923 to determine the legality of the transaction and to maintain proper records of the transaction.

Generally, 18 U.S.C. § 922 prohibits the sale of a firearm to a person who,
- (a) has been convicted of a misdemeanor crime of domestic violence;
- (b) has been convicted of a felony, or any other crime, punishable by imprisonment for a term exceeding one year (this does not include state misdemeanors punishable by imprisonment of two years or less);
- (c) is a fugitive from justice;
- (d) is an unlawful user of, or addicted to, marijuana or any depressant, stimulant, or narcotic drug, or any other controlled substance;
- (e) has been adjudicated mentally defective or has been committed to a mental institution;
- (f) has been discharged from the armed forces under dishonorable conditions;
- (g) has renounced his or her US citizenship;
- (h) is an alien illegally in the United States under a nonimmigrant visa;
- (i) is subject to certain restraining orders; or
- (j) is under indictment or information for a felony, or any other crime, punishable by imprisonment for a term exceeding one year.

Chapter 3

Types of Ammunition

We deal in lead, friend.
Steve McQueen, *The Magnificent Seven* (1960)

Chapter 3 provides a description of the basic characteristics and types of handgun ammunition, along with numerical data on ballistic performance, and identifies some well-known ammunition suppliers.

By definition, ammunition includes cartridge cases, primers, bullets, or propellant powder designed for use in any firearm (18 U.S.C. § 921). Handgun ammunition may be classified as either rimfire or centerfire depending upon where the primer is located in the cartridge.

Suggested reading:

Forker, Bob. 2013. *Ammo and Ballistics for Hunters, Shooters, and Collectors.* 5th ed. Long Beach, California: Safari Press.

Barnes, Frank C. 2006. *Cartridges of the World.* 11th ed. Iola, Wisconsin: Gun Digest Books.

Bullets

A bullet is a projectile that is usually made of lead, sometimes covered with a layer of copper or other metal, and is located at the mouth of the cartridge case. Bullets may be characterized as soft nose, hollow point, or full metal jacket.

Types of Ammunition

Soft-nose bullets are nonexpanding bullets that rapidly transfer energy to the target upon impact.

Hollow-point bullets have a cavity in the nose to aid in expansion at impact.

Full-metal-jacket bullets allow for higher muzzle velocities than unjacketed lead bullets and are more useful against hard targets.

Bullet Weight

The *grain* is the unit of measure of projectile (or bullet) weight in ammunition. On a box of loaded ammunition, the grain value is generally shown along with the caliber and type of bullet designation (e.g., .45 ACP, 230 grains, FMJ) Example: Given that one grain equals 0.0648 grams or 64.8 milligrams, then a bullet weighing 230 grains weighs 14.9 grams.

Caliber

Caliber is a numerical term that is a rough approximation of the bullet diameter. It is commonly expressed in hundredths of an inch (e.g., .45 caliber) or in millimeters (e.g., 9 mm). For example, a .45-caliber bullet is approximately half an inch in diameter. Caliber describes the specific size bullet that can be fired by a specific firearm. Individuals just starting to shoot firearms need to be very careful to use the correct caliber ammunition for which a handgun is intended. Below is a table that lists the most common types of handgun ammunition calibers and the year that they were introduced for usage.

Types of Ammunition

Table 12. Common Handgun Cartridge Calibers

Cartridge Caliber	Year
.22 LR	1887
.22 Winchester Magnum	1959
.25 ACP (6.35 mm)	1908
.32 ACP (7.65 mm)	1899
.357 Magnum	1935
.357 SIG	1994
.380 ACP (9 mm Short)	1912
.38 S&W Special	1902
.40 S&W	1989
.41 Remington Magnum	1964
.44 S&W Special	1907
.44 Remington Magnum	1955
.45 Long Colt	1873
.45 ACP (aka .45 Auto)	1905
.45 GAP	2003
.454 Casull	1957
.460 S&W Magnum	2005
.480 Ruger	2003
.50 Auto Express	1991
9x19 mm Luger (Parabellum)	1902
10 mm Auto	1983

Source: *NRA Sourcebook, et al.*

Types of Bullets

Here is an alphabetical list of acronyms and terms that are commonly used to describe various types of bullets.

- ACP: Acronym for Automatic Colt Pistol. Used in conjunction with cartridge caliber designations (for example, a .45 ACP cartridge).
- AP: Armor-piercing. See section below for definition of armor-piercing bullets.
- Ball: Refers to a bullet that is fully jacketed. These bullets are nonexpanding, have a greater penetration compared to hollow points, and are not recommended for concealed carry. See *FMJ*.
- Centerfire: A type of cartridge that has the primer centrally located in the base of the case.
- CorBon: Cor®Bon is the trademark name of the CorBon Custom Bullet Company in Sturgis, South Dakota. The company was founded in 1982 by Peter Pi Sr., a developer of hunting cartridges. The company's name is derived from their unique core-bonding process that chemically bonds the lead core to the jacket of a bullet, creating a fused bullet. Today CorBon Company is also a premium supplier of self-defense ammunition. CorBon offers a broad line of high-performance handgun ammunition in calibers ranging from .32 Auto through .454 Casull. CorBon handgun bullets are top of the line, having higher muzzle velocities and energies than are typical of the more common loads for a given caliber.
- Dummy round: A round that contains a bullet but does not contain a primer or a powder charge and therefore cannot be fired.
- FMJ (bullet): Acronym for *full-metal-jacketed* bullet. A bullet consisting of a lead core completely covered, except for the base, with a copper alloy jacket, approximately 90 percent copper and 10 percent zinc (US DoJ/NIJ 2001). A FMJ bullet is a nonexpanding

bullet and transfers less energy to a target than an expanding hollow-point bullet of the same caliber and weight. A FMJ bullet generally has less stopping power and a greater chance of overpenetration than a comparable hollow-point bullet. Therefore, FMJ bullets are recommended for target shooting practice, while *jacketed-hollow point* (JHP) bullets are recommended for concealed carry and self-defense.

- GAP: Acronym for the Glock Automatic Pistol .45-caliber cartridge introduced in 2003 for its Glock Model 37 handgun. The .45 GAP cartridge is a shortened version of the .45 ACP cartridge.

- Hollow point: A bullet with a cavity in the nose to aid in expansion at impact and penetration. A bullet with a hollow point has potentially greater stopping power because it distorts and expands at impact and leaves a bigger hole than a nonexpanding bullet. Hollow-point bullets inflict greater damage to the target and are the best choice for self-defense. See *stopping power*.

- JHP (bullet): Acronym for *jacketed hollow-point* bullet. A bullet consisting of a lead core that has a hollow cavity or hole located in the nose and that is completely covered, except for the hollow point, with a copper-alloy jacket containing approximately 90 percent copper and 10 percent zinc (US DoJ/NIJ 2001). Jacketed hollow-point bullets are recommended for personal protection and self-defense because they expand upon impact, transfer energy within the target very efficiently, and have much less chance of overpenetration. See *hollow point*.

- JSP (bullet): Acronym for *jacketed soft-point* bullet. A lead bullet, also known as a semijacketed soft point (SJSP), completely covered, except for the point, with a copper-alloy jacket, approximately 90 percent copper and 10 percent zinc (US DoJ/NIJ 2001). This type of bullet expands and provides better terminal performance when compared to solid lead and FMJ bullets. However, soft-point bullets are more popular for hunting and are not considered as effective as hollow-point bullets for personal defense. The JSP bullet is good for indoor ranges because it penetrates less than FMJ bullets and is safer than lead bullets. See *SJSP*.

- JTC (bullet): Acronym for *jacketed truncated cone*. A bullet with a cone-shaped nose with the end cut off so that it has a flat tip and that is partially or fully covered by a metal such as copper. This type of bullet is good for target shooting and competition matches because it leaves a round hole in paper targets, making it easier to score. The metal jacket that covers the lead is for safety reasons and prevents exposure to lead while handling. A JTC bullet may be more prone to feed reliability problems.

- Lead bullet: A bullet made entirely of lead, which may be alloyed with hardening agents. Lead bullets are nonexpanding and are not recommended for concealed carry. Lead bullets may also result in lead accumulation problems with some pistols after repeated firings. All lead bullets without a jacket covering are less safe to handle because the lead may get on your hands. See *nonexpanding bullets*.

- Magnum: A term used to describe a cartridge that is generally larger and that produces a higher velocity and energy than standard cartridges of a given caliber. Magnum ammunition has greater penetration capability than standard ammunition. Two common examples are the .357 Magnum and the .44 Magnum cartridges.

- MC: Acronym for *metal cased, metallic coating*, or *metal clad*. Basically, it is a bullet that has a complete metal covering. A MC bullet is the same as a FMJ bullet. See *FMJ*.

- Nonexpanding bullets: Nonexpanding or non-hollow-point bullets include full-metal-jacketed (FMJ), semiwadcutter (SWC), wadcutter (WC), round-nose-lead (RNL), and jacketed-soft-point (JSP) bullets. All of these solid bullets have serious disadvantages compared to hollow-point bullets for self-defense. Specifically, nonexpanding bullets have less stopping power because less energy is transferred to the target, and they have a much greater chance of overpenetration, which can lead to collateral damage or unintended fatalities. Experts generally do not recommend nonexpanding bullets for self-protection because of these drawbacks.

- Parabellum: Latin word meaning "prepare for war" normally used in describing a certain type of 9 mm cartridge (i.e., 9 mm Parabellum). Parabellum was also a trademark for various weapons manufactured by Deutsche Waffen & Munitionsfabrik (DWM) in Berlin, Germany. Georg Luger developed a new semiautomatic pistol that was marketed as a Parabellum and that eventually became known as a Luger. The first Luger pistol was chambered for a 7.65 mm Parabellum cartridge. The 9 mm Luger (Parabellum) cartridge was developed in 1902.

- Plus P (+P): Designation for cartridges that are loaded to higher pressures than standard ammunition. For example, standard pressure for a .38 Special cartridge is around 17,000 pounds per square inch (psi). A .38 Special +P cartridge will average around 18,500 psi.

- Plus P plus (+P+): Designation for cartridges that are loaded to higher pressures than +P ammunition. A .38-caliber +P+ cartridge has an average pressure around 22,000 psi.

- Rimfire: A rimfire cartridge has the chemical compound of the primer located inside the rim of the cartridge case. Most rimfire ammunition for handguns is .22 caliber.

- Round nose (RN bullet): A bullet with a blunt or rounded nose, or a bullet with a generally blunt or rounded nose or tip, that possesses a small, flat surface at the tip (NIJ 2001).

- SJHP (bullet): Acronym for *semijacketed-hollow-point* bullet. A bullet consisting of a lead core with a copper-alloy (approximately 90 percent copper and 10 percent zinc) jacket covering the base and bore riding surface (major diameter), that leaves some portion of the lead core exposed, thus forming a lead nose or tip that has a hollow cavity or hole located in it (NIJ 2001). See *JHP*.
- SJSP (bullet): Acronym for *semijacketed-soft-point* bullet. A bullet, also known as a jacketed soft point (JSP), consisting of a lead core with a copper-alloy (approximately 90 percent copper and 10 percent zinc) jacket covering the base and bore riding surface (major diameter), that leaves some portion of the lead core exposed, thus forming a lead nose or tip (NIJ 2001). See *JSP*.
- Semiwadcutter (SWC): A bullet having both a flat point and a pronounced, sharp shoulder. Semiwadcutter bullets are used for target shooting because they cut very clean holes in paper targets.
- Wadcutter (WC): A type of bullet having a completely flat front surface that extends to the full bullet diameter and that is designed to punch a clean hole in a target. A flat-nosed wadcutter bullet is often used in a revolver for gun matches because it produces sharp, round holes in the target. See *semiwadcutter*.
- Winchester Magnum Rimfire (WMR): The .22-caliber WMR is a .22-caliber rimfire cartridge (also known as .22 Magnum) originally introduced in 1959 for rifles but also currently used in handguns. The case of a .22 WMR bullet is thicker than that of the .22 LR bullet, allowing high pressures that provide up to 1,500 feet per second velocity.
- X-Panding bullets: CorBon Custom Bullet Company introduced a trademark Deep Penetrating X-Panding (DPX) bullet in 2004. Today CorBon offers a line of DPX handgun ammunition for self-defense in calibers ranging from .32 Auto through .454 Casull. These high-

performance ammunition cartridges have higher muzzle velocity and muzzle energy than is typical of the more standard loads of each caliber.

Range of Bullets (Maximum)

Typical handgun bullets have maximum ranges of approximately one to one and a half miles. Therefore, it is very important to know your target and the backstop.

Table 13. Typical Maximum Range of Selected Bullets

Cartridge (caliber)	Weight (grains)	Velocity (feet/sec)	Range (feet)
.22 LR	40	1,255	4,870
.38 Special +P	158	890	6,400
9 mm Luger	123	1,120	5,700
.357 Magnum	158	1,235	7,100
.45 ACP	230	855	4,400
.44 Magnum	240	1,390	7,500

Source: *NRA Firearms Fact Book.*

One mile = 5,280 feet

As a matter of firearm safety you must be sure that the bullets you are shooting at an outdoor range will not travel beyond the firing range and hit something they shouldn't.

Armor Piercing Bullets

Armor-piercing (AP) ammunition is intended primarily for penetrating metal or body armor. Armor-piercing ammunition for pistols is banned from the general public by federal law at 18 U.S.C. § 921(a)(7). The United States Code at 18 U.S.C. § 921, 17B (i) & (ii)] defines armor-piercing ammunition as follows:

Types of Ammunition

B) The term "armor piercing ammunition" means - (i) a projectile or projectile core which may be used in a handgun and which is constructed entirely (excluding the presence of traces of other substances) from one or a combination of tungsten alloys, steel, iron, brass, bronze, beryllium copper, or depleted uranium; or (ii) a full jacketed projectile larger than .22 caliber designed and intended for use in a handgun and whose jacket has a weight of more than 25 percent of the total weight of the projectile.

The State of Florida defines "armor piercing bullet" as any bullet that has a steel inner core or core of equivalent hardness and a truncated cone and that is designed for use in a handgun as an armor-piercing or metal-piercing bullet (Florida Statute 790.31).

Selected Ammunition Suppliers

This section lists in alphabetical order six popular manufacturers of ammunition in the US. Each company supplies ammunition intended for concealed-carry handguns for self-defense. For a more detailed look at the manufacturers' ammunition, I recommend visiting their websites or obtaining a copy of their most recent catalog of ammunition. CorBon is known as a supplier of very high performance ammunition.

CorBon

CORBON/Glaser
1311 Industry Rd
Sturgis, SD 57785
(800) 626-7266
www.corbon.com

Federal Premium Ammunition

Federal Cartridge Company
900 Ehlen Drive
Anoka, MN 55303-7503
(800) 322-2342
www.federal premium.com

Hornady

Hornady Manufacturing Company
3625 West Old Potash Hwy
Grand Island, NE 68803
(800)338-3220
www.hornady.com

Remington

Ammunition & Components Plant
2592 Arkansas Hwy 15 N
Lonoke, AR 72086
(501) 676-3161
www.remington.com

Speer

Speer Ammo
2299 Snake River Avenue
Lewiston, ID 83501
(800) 256-8685
www.speer-ammo.com

Winchester

Winchester Repeating Arms
275 Winchester Avenue
Morgan, UT 84050
(800) 333-3288
www.winchester.com

Chapter 4

Ammunition Evaluation

*If a gunman has to be killed in a crowd, a hollow-point
expanding bullet that will not go through his body and hit a
bystander is the best to use.*
Elmer Keith, *Six Guns* (1955)

Ammunition evaluation refers to the process of testing
and evaluating various calibers of ammunition to determine
their stopping-power effectiveness or ability to incapacitate an
aggressor. Evaluation of ammunition includes considerations
of muzzle velocity and energy, stopping power, energy
transfer, bullet penetration, and various mathematical
incapacitation indices.

Chapter 4 describes various methods used to evaluate
ammunition effectiveness, specifically, ballistic firing of
bullets into gelatin, real-world gunfights, and various
mathematical formulas. The work of various experts is
summarized to provide a basic understanding of the criteria
that are used to select ammunition for self-defense. The time
periods of most of the evaluations occurred within the past 50
years, but there is reference to some that go back even further
(e.g., Elmer Keith).

Suggested reading:

Marshall, Evan P., and Edwin J. Sanow. 2001. *Stopping Power: A Practical Analysis of the Latest Handgun Ammunition.* Boulder, Colorado: Paladin Press.

Keith, Elmer. (1961) 2013. "Selection of Cartridges." Chap. 18 in *Six Guns: The Standard Reference Work*, 275–289. Reprint. Lexington, Kentucky: Sportsman's Vintage Press.

Muzzle Velocity

The velocity of a projectile upon exiting the muzzle of the handgun, usually expressed in feet per second (ft/sec) or meters per second (m/s). See also *muzzle energy*. The muzzle velocities and muzzle energies of common handgun ammunition are listed in Table 14.

Ammunition Evaluation

Table 14. Muzzle Velocities and Energies of Selected
Ammunition (Source: *Gun Digest, 2015)*

Cartridge (caliber)	Weight (grains)	Velocity (ft/sec)	Energy (ft-lb)
.380 Auto	60	1,130	170
.380 Auto	100	955	190
.38 Special	158	755	200
.38 Special +P	158	890	280
9 mm Luger	90	1,360	370
9 mm Luger	95	1,300	350
9 mm Luger	100	1,180	305
9 mm	115	1,280	420
10 mm FBI	180	950	361
.40 S&W	155	1,140	447
.40 S&W	180	985	388
.45 ACP	230	830	355
.45 ACP	185	1,000	410
.45 ACP +P	185	1,140	535
.45 GAP	230	880	396
.45 GAP	185	1,090	490
.357 Magnum	110	1,295	410
.357 Magnum	158	1,235	535
.357 Magnum	180	1,180	557
.357 SIG	125	1,350	510
.44 Magnum	180	1,610	1,035
.44 Magnum	240	1,180	740
.22 LR	40	1,070	100

General Conclusions:

(1) Comparing +P loads to standard loads for the same caliber and bullet weights (see .38 Special and .45 ACP), the +P bullets have higher velocity and higher muzzle energy.

48

(2) The muzzle energy of .40 S&W is generally higher than 9 mm Luger, one of the factors in law enforcement's move toward the .40 S&W after the Miami shootout.

(3) In terms of muzzle energies, the .380 Auto and .38 Special cartridges are "anemic" compared to all others except .22 LR.

(4) The 180-grain .44 Magnum bullet is approximately ten times more powerful than the 40-grain .22 LR bullet.

(5) Lighter-weight bullets generally have higher muzzle velocities and energies than heavier bullets of the same caliber (e.g., 185- vs. 230-grain .45 ACP; 90-, 95-, and 100 grain 9 mm Luger)

Note: In *Stopping Power*, Marshall and Sanow report that when comparing muzzle energy to stopping power, the most effective rounds have muzzle energies of at least 400 ft-lb.

Muzzle Energy

The kinetic energy of a projectile upon exiting the muzzle of a handgun, usually expressed in foot-pounds of energy (ft-lb) or joules (J).

Example: The muzzle energy of a bullet (in foot-pounds[1]) can be calculated if the weight of the bullet (in grains) and the muzzle velocity (in feet per second) are known, using the following equation:

Energy = (bullet weight) * (velocity)^2 / 450,400
Given: .44 Magnum caliber
Bullet weight = 180 grains
Muzzle velocity = 1,610 feet per second

---

1. A foot-pound is defined as a unit of work or energy equal to the work done when a force of one pound moves a distance of one foot. One foot-pound equals 1.35 joules.

Muzzle energy = (180) (1,610)^2 / 450,400 = 1,035 ft-lb

Kinetic energy is the energy associated with motion. Many experts believe that there is a minimum energy level of 400 ft-lb of kinetic energy (i.e., muzzle energy) that a bullet must possess if it is to be an effective round that will reliably incapacitate an aggressor. Energy levels of between 450 and 550 ft-lb have been proven effective for many decades in real-world gunfights. The equation in physics that is used for determining kinetic energy is as follows:

Kinetic energy = (mass) x (velocity)^2 / 2

Stopping Power

The term *stopping power* refers to the capability of a bullet or a gun to incapacitate an assailant to prevent further aggression. Stopping power is a complex and somewhat controversial subject among handgun experts. There are a variety of mathematical formulas and techniques that have been used as measures of stopping-power effectiveness based upon bullet caliber, shape, weight, and velocity. Specific examples include the Hatcher relative stopping power (RSP), Taylor knock-out factor (TKOF), relative incapacitation index (RII), and the Fuller index. There have also been a lot of ballistic tests conducted to determine how far specific bullets penetrate into ballistic gelatin; another measure of stopping power.

According to Marshall and Sanow, "Stopping power is not hard to understand. It is simply a matter of energy transfer. Bullets that transfer the most energy...produce the most stopping power." Another school of thought supported extensively in the literature by Dr. Martin Fackler considers wound ballistics essential to any discussion of stopping power. The Fackler school of thought regards a deep permanent wound channel, not quick energy transfer, as essential to stopping power.

Physiological and neurological factors are also important. According to Dr. W. French Anderson, who did the forensic analysis of the FBI Miami shootout, the two most effective ways to stop an aggressor instantly are (a) to take out the brain or upper spinal cord that controls the nervous system or (b) to put a major tear or hole in the heart or aorta to stop the heart from functioning. In his view, the real measure of stopping power of a handgun bullet depends upon the bullet's ability to disrupt vital bodily functions. An accurate shot with sufficient energy to penetrate the heart or brain is the most effective stopper of all. See *Muzzle Energy* and *Taylor Knock-out Factor*.

When comparing muzzle energy to stopping power, Marshall and Sanow found that rounds with at least 400 ft-lb of muzzle energy are the most effective one-shot stoppers. The effectiveness of various calibers of selected ammunition is shown in Table 15.

Table 15. One-Shot-Stop Effectiveness of Selected Bullet Calibers (Expressed in Percent)

Bullet caliber	Bullet weight (grains)	Bullet type	Muzzle energy (ft-lb)	%
9 mm	115	JHP+P+	432	93
9 mm	147	JHP	295	78
.40 S&W	155	JHP	495	97
.40 S&W	180	JHP	360	80
.357 Magnum	125	JHP	580	96
.45 ACP	185	JHP	423	90
.380 ACP	90	JHP	200	69
.38 Spec (2")	125	JHP+P	248	66

Ammunition Evaluation

Source: Marshall, Evan P., and Edwin J. Sanow. 2001. *Stopping Power: A Practical Analysis of the Latest Handgun Ammunition.* Boulder, CO: Paladin Press.

Marshall and Sanow's book is a comprehensive and state-of-the art assessment of the stopping power of various bullets based upon gelatin ballistic tests and real-world gunfights. This book is for those who want to get into the details and history of stopping-power methods and the effectiveness of various-caliber bullets.

In his book *Combat Handgunnery* (1997), Chuck Taylor assesses various methods used to evaluate the stopping power of handgun cartridges during the 1970s, '80s, and '90s. He describes the Hatcher and Taylor methods for determining relative stopping power, the National Institute of Justice/Law Enforcement Assistance Administration relative incapacitation index (RII), and Dr. Martin Fackler's analysis based on wound ballistics. He discusses the controversies in the methods for determining stopping power up to that time.

Taylor himself developed a mathematical formula based on various bullet characteristics including bullet weight, velocity, shape, and cross-sectional area:

$T = WAVY / 1,000$ where T is a Taylor number measure of stopping power, W is the bullet weight, A is the bullet cross-sectional area, V is the bullet velocity, and Y is a form factor. ($Y = 1.25$ if $V > 1,088$ ft/sec or $Y = 1.00$ if $V < 1,088$ ft/sec)

Using the Taylor formula, a passing score for stopping power effectiveness is 20 or higher. Results for three different-caliber bullets are shown below:

.45 ACP/185 grains: Taylor score = 41
9 mm/115 grains: Taylor score = 17
.38 Special/158 grains: Taylor score = 14

Suggested reading:

Taylor, Chuck. 1997. *Combat Handgunnery*. 4th ed. Iola, Wisconsin: Krause, 42–52.

Incapacitation

In the context of a self-defense encounter, incapacitation is the rendering of an assailant or aggressor unable to continue the aggression. To incapacitate an assailant most effectively requires that the brain, spinal cord, or heart be made nonfunctional (see *stopping power*). For a more complete treatment, see John Jacobs in Marshall and Sanow, pages 217–219.

Adams, et al. in *Street Survival* reported that one liquor store robber was shot thirty-three times with 9 mm rounds before becoming incapacitated.

In another self-defense shooting (Waters, 1998), a woman in Cape Coral, Florida, shot an assailant with a .25-caliber semiautomatic pistol loaded with four soft-nosed bullets. The first shot entered his mouth, the second hit him in the heart, the third went into the assailant's abdomen, and the final shot hit him in the groin. Despite being hit four times in critical places, the attacker continued beating the woman for several minutes before finally collapsing. This is another example of a situation where a low-caliber handgun was ineffective as a self-defense weapon. It took way too long to incapacitate the assailant.

Taylor Knock-Out Factor (TKOF)

John "Pondoro" Taylor (1904-1969) was a big-game African hunter who experimented with different types and calibers of firearms and developed a mathematical approach for evaluating the "stopping power" of various cartridges. This measure of effectiveness became known as the Taylor KO Factor and is calculated as follows:

TKOF = (mass) x (velocity) x (diameter) / 7,000

Bullet mass is in grains
Bullet velocity is in feet per second
Bullet diameter is in inches
Example:
*Winchester 9 mm Luger 115-grain silver-tip hollow-point (STHP) bullet
TKOF = (115) x (1,225) x (.380) / 7,000 = 7.6

*This bullet was selected as representative of the one that critically wounded Michael Platt during the FBI Miami shootout of 1986, but it did not instantly incapacitate Platt, and he was able to kill the FBI agent who shot him.

For comparison purposes, typical Taylor KO factors for three other-caliber bullets are listed below:

Caliber .40 S&W: TKO = 10
Caliber .45 Auto: TKO = 11
Caliber .357 Magnum: TKO = 10
(Source: Forker, Bob. 2013.)

Fuller Index

Evan Marshall and programmer Steve Fuller analyzed data from 13,500 shootings and developed a method for estimating one-shot stopping-power effectiveness. The parameter that resulted is known as the Fuller index, expressed as a percentage of one-shot stops based upon actual shooting results. The Fuller index is used for predicting the stopping power of bullets from .22 caliber to .44 Magnum. It is calculated from the initial diameter and muzzle energy of the bullet, and its penetration depth in 10 percent gelatin. The

Fuller index represents another method for predicting the stopping power of bullets.

Bullet Penetration

Bullet penetration of ballistic gelatin is one measure of stopping power commonly studied. At one time, ammunition experts strived for penetration distances of eighteen to twenty inches in ballistic gelatin. The newer criterion for penetration is nine inches for the acceptable minimum and up to fifteen inches maximum. The new criterion optimizes energy transfer in the target and minimizes overpenetration that could cause unintended fatalities or injuries (Marshall and Sanow 2001).

Marshall and Sanow in 2001 reported the following key findings regarding the penetration of bullets:

(1) The amount of energy transferred to a target in the first twelve inches is the key to stopping power. Bullets that penetrate deeper than twelve inches produce much less stopping power.
(2) Hollow-point bullets transfer 95 percent of their energy in the first twelve inches of gelatin. Solid bullets transfer an average of just 63 percent of their energy in the first twelve inches of gelatin.
(3) Hollow-point bullets in 9 mm, .357 Magnum, .357 SIG, .40 S&W, and .45 ACP all transfer 350 to 500 ft-lb of energy in penetrating twelve inches of gelatin.
(4) FMJ, RNL, and SWC bullets are very likely to overpenetrate a human target. The US Border Patrol selected twelve inches for their protocol because that is considered the depth of the average human torso.
(5) In addition to poor stopping power, nearly all nonexpanding bullets have another serious problem— overpenetration. Bullets that penetrate more than twelve inches are likely to exit a torso.

The fundamental conclusion from penetration studies in ballistic gelatin is that hollow-point bullets are preferred for self-defense over nonexpanding bullets because hollow points have better stopping power and are much less likely to overpenetrate.

An example of bullet overpenetration is documented in a report by Edgewood Arsenal (March 1965) regarding the wound ballistics of 160-grain 6.5 mm Mannlicher-Carcano rifle ball ammunition with a gilding metal jacket. Ballistic tests using gelatin determined that bullet exit velocities merely lost on average about 125 feet per second after passing through 13.5 centimeters of gelatin. Bullets having an average striking velocity of 1,900 feet per second after being firing from 60 yards were reduced to an average exit velocity of 1,775 feet per second.

This US Army ballistics study confirmed that it was very possible that the bullet that struck President Kennedy in the neck could have also been responsible for Governor Connally's wounds. This was the conclusion of the Warren Commission that investigated the JFK assassination. This ballistic test study is cited here as an example of overpenetration of full-metal-jacket ball ammunition with significant exit velocity (Olivier and Dziemian 1965).

FBI Miami Shootout

On April 11, 1986, two FBI agents were killed and five more wounded in a shootout in Miami, Florida, with two armed robbers who were also shot and killed. The FBI agents outnumbered the bad guys four to one, yet they suffered multiple casualties. The subsequent FBI investigation blamed the excessive casualties in part on the lack of stopping power of their 9 mm handguns and their Caliber .38 +P rounds, and the difficulty of reloading their .357 Magnum revolvers.

Michael Platt was one of the armed robbers killed in the shootout. The gunshot wound that was primarily responsible for his death due to blood loss was caused by a 9 mm bullet fired by FBI agent Jerry Dove from approximately thirty feet away. Dove was also subsequently killed.

According to Dr. W. French Anderson's forensic analysis of the shooting, Dove's 9 mm Winchester Silvertip round penetrated right up to, but stopped just short of, Platt's heart. It is believed that, had that bullet penetrated his heart, Platt would have died more quickly, and the gunfight would have ended at that point, with only one injury sustained by the FBI agents.

The official report states that a caliber .38+P Special round would probably *not* have penetrated Platt's rib cage, whereas .40-, .45- or .357-caliber bullets would probably have killed Platt instantly. This incident led the FBI to evaluate more powerful handguns with more stopping power.

Suggested reading:

Anderson, W. French. 2006. *Forensic Analysis of the April 11, 1986, FBI Firefight*. Boulder, Colorado: Paladin Press.

In the aftermath of this incident, the FBI began an effort to increase the effectiveness of their handgun firepower. For a few years, the FBI began testing 10 mm caliber semiauto handguns, but their excessive recoil and muzzle flash were undesirable characteristics. To solve these problems, Federal Cartridge Company supplied a downloaded 10 mm cartridge known as "FBI Lite" that was milder in recoil and had less muzzle flash.

Then Smith & Wesson took a step further and shortened the FBI Lite cartridge case and it became known as "10 mm short" because of its reduced case size. This ultimately led to the introduction of a new round of ammunition, the .40 S&W caliber cartridge in 1989 (Kasler 1992).

Since then the .40 S&W cartridge has become widely adopted by law enforcement departments. Performance-wise the .40 S&W used in modern semiauto handguns is generally more powerful than a 9 mm cartridge and does not have the recoil or flash of the 10 mm cartridge.

The use of revolvers by the FBI, as opposed to semi-autos, in the Miami shootout was a detriment because it was difficult to reload them. One of the reasons for the high usage of semiauto handguns by law enforcement today is because they are easier and quicker to reload than revolvers, and can generally hold more rounds of ammunition.

In recent years (2014-2016) there are indications that some law enforcement agencies are making a switch back to 9 mm-caliber handguns. The FBI has indicated plans to switch from .40-caliber Glocks to 9 mm Glock pistols. The Georgia State Police (GSP) have already gone to 9 mm Glocks after a stint with the .45 GAP Glock 37 (Glock 2016, 52).

New advances in handgun ammunition have improved the stopping power of 9 mm cartridges, such that they are comparable to larger service calibers in penetration and generation of wound channels. In particular, the GSP have found the 124-grain Gold Dot +P bullet to be an effective round. Other police departments that have recently starting using caliber 9 x 19 mm Glock 17 Gen 4 pistols for service include the Grand Rapids PD in Michigan, the Mississippi Highway Patrol, and the Castle Rock PD in Colorado (Glock 2016, 52-73).

US Border Patrol

The US Border Patrol is a federal law enforcement agency under the Department of Homeland Security whose mission is to prevent the entry into the United States of illegal aliens, drug traffickers, and terrorists. Border Patrol agents throughout their history have been engaged in many gunfights. As a consequence, they have gained a great deal of experience with various types of ammunition and have been leaders in the testing and evaluation of ammunition to determine their stopping-power effectiveness.

John Jacobs, a career law enforcement officer and firearms instructor, provides a detailed history of the handgun ammunition used by the US Border Patrol from 1970 to 2000 in chapter 25 of the book *Stopping Power* (2001). Since Border Patrol agents have been involved in so many gunfights throughout the years, what they use for handgun ammunition and how they arrived at their current choice of ammunition can be very instructive to other law enforcement agencies and to anyone who carries a concealed handgun for self-protection.

Here I summarize the lessons learned from the Border Patrol and make my own obvious conclusions from their evaluation. The US Border Patrol has used the following ammunition rounds in service at various times in its history as indicated in Table 16.

Table 16. US Border Patrol History of Ammunition Usage

Caliber and Description of Bullet	Approximate Timeframe
.45 ACP Ball	?
.38 Special RNL	1950s
.357 Magnum 158-grain JSP	1970s
.38 Special +P+ 110-grain JHP	1982-1986
.357 Magnum 110-grain JHP	From 1984
.38 Super JHP	?
9 mm +P+ 115-grain JHP	From 1987
.40 S&W 155-grain JHP	From 1994

Source: Jacobs 2001

The most obvious conclusion is that the US Border Patrol agents transitioned from nonexpanding bullets (i.e., ball, round-nose lead, and soft point) to expanding jacketed hollow-point (JHP) bullets. The ammunition evaluation over the decades was focused on optimizing various parameters and making tradeoffs. In general, the goal of their evaluation was to optimize energy transfer to the target to maximize stopping power or incapacitation potential; keep recoil and handling characteristics within acceptable limits for the users; and avoid less effective, overpenetrating rounds that could potentially harm bystanders. The last indication in this report is that the .40 S&W–caliber 155-grain bullet was selected as the favorite.

The choice of .40 S&W caliber is consistent with Ed Sanow's observation in 2001 that police departments had been looking at .40 S&W and .357 SIG to replace worn-out firearms and for new procurements. Today .40 S&W is widely selected by many law enforcement agencies, although as stated above, the 9 mm cartridge is still competitive due to improvements and it appears to be making a comeback.

Wound Ballistics

Wound ballistics is a field of study concerning the effects on the body produced by penetrating projectiles. Martin L. Fackler, MD, was a leading expert in the field of wound ballistics. He has written extensively on projectile-tissue interactions and has been critical of much of the work in the literature regarding stopping power.

Dr. Fackler was a staunch advocate of the scientific method and identified what he thought were misconceptions concerning the focus on bullet velocity and kinetic energy transfer in predicting wound ballistics. The focus in wound ballistics is on the permanent and temporary cavities produced when a projectile impacts tissue.

I do not attempt to favor any school of stopping-power theory or empirical evidence advocated by the sources I refer to in this book. I only point out the complexity, controversy, and uncertainty that has evolved in this field among various experts. Some experts favor scientific, reproducible ballistic test results using ballistic gelatin. Others prefer to favor empirical results from actual shootings. Still others emphasize that wound ballistics is the only valid criterion.

It would appear that each approach has some degree of validity, and there is no absolute answer. It must be noted that stopping effectiveness is also dependent and significantly affected by the accuracy of placement on the target.

Suggested reading:

Fackler, M. L. 1987, July. *What's Wrong with the Wound Ballistics Literature, and Why*. Institute Report No. 239, Letterman Army Institute of Research. (Presidio of San Francisco). (http://www.rkba.org/research/fackler/wrong.html)

Patrick, Urey W. 1989. "Handgun Wounding Factors and Effectiveness." Quantico, Virginia: FBI Academy, July 14. (http://gundata.org/images/fbi-handgun-ballistics.pdf)

Elmer Keith

Elmer Merrifield Keith (1899–1984) was a firearms enthusiast and author who was instrumental in the development of the first magnum revolver cartridge, the .357 Magnum, as well as the .44 Magnum and .41 Magnum cartridges that came later. His classic book *Six Guns* was originally published in 1955.

In chapter 15 of *Six Guns*, "Gunfighting," Elmer Keith describes a variety of real gunfight shootouts. In one case, a friend of his named Lieutenant Williamson of the Jacksonville Police Department emptied his .38 Special handgun into the chest of a crazed man wielding a razor. The man kept coming at him until he shot him again right between the eyes with a .44 Special bullet.

Keith reports numerous other gunfights and concludes that nothing short of .357 Magnum, .44 Special, .45 Colt, or .45 Auto firepower is needed for reliable defense (Keith 1955).

You might consider Elmer Keith to be yet another school of thought regarding stopping power; that is, what I might call "old school." As the saying goes, those who do not remember the past are condemned to repeat it, so why not consider specifically what Elmer Keith had to say about the stopping power of various cartridges? Below are a few quotes excerpted with permission from *Six Guns*.

Elmer Keith on .38 Special Cartridges

Quote from *Six Guns*:

> Thirty-eight Specials have proved inadequate in
> so many gun fights that there is no doubt as to
> their inferiority in comparison to the larger and
> more powerful calibers. We could fill a chapter
> with cases where criminals took from one to six
> shots from standard .38 Specials and stayed on
> their feet and kept fighting, often to the demise
> of a police officer.

As the above quote from Elmer Keith states, .38-caliber
handguns are not the most effective manstoppers. A historic
event involving Teddy Roosevelt provides one more example
of the lack of stopping power of .38-caliber bullets. While
campaigning in Milwaukee in 1912, Teddy Roosevelt was shot
by would-be assassin John Schrank with a .38 Special S&W
revolver.

The bullet passed through Roosevelt's double-folded
speech papers and his eyeglass case and lodged inside his chest
cavity. Roosevelt did not get immediate medical attention to
remove the bullet and went on to give his speech unscathed. At
least in this case, the outcome was favorable because Schrank
failed.

Elmer Keith on .357 Magnum

Quote from *Six Guns*:

> This is the only .38 caliber cartridge, really
> .357 of an inch, that we consider an adequate
> man-stopper. It is also effective for game
> shooting, including moose, elk, grizzly bear,

mule deer, and antelope, using a 158 grain bullet at 1,300 to 1,400 feet per second.

Elmer Keith on .45 Calibers

Quote from *Six Guns*:

> In the auto pistol the old .45 Colt auto service cartridge with 230 grain bullet at velocities of 800 to 850 feet per second is the best man-stopper of all the auto-loading pistol cartridges. For the man who prefers the auto pistol, the .45 auto will deliver the goods as a man-stopper or on game, better than any smaller auto cartridge. The 9 mm calibers and even the more powerful Super 38 all lack stopping power in comparison to the .45 auto.

Suggested reading:

Keith, Elmer. (1961) 2013. *Six Guns: The Standard Reference Work*. Reprint. Lexington, Kentucky: Sportsman's Vintage Press.

Elmer Keith's accounts were based on events that occurred during the first half of the last century. He provides some interesting historical perspective. However, since then ammunition and handgun improvements have occurred so his anecdotal observations need to be put in context.

A Case for .22 Caliber

Throughout this chapter I make a case for higher-caliber ammunition for self-defense. Here I make a case for the .22 WMR, a small-caliber bullet that provides some degree of self-protection. A .22-caliber WMR handgun, despite its small caliber, may still have a role in personal protection and self-defense. Such a handgun offers low recoil, light weight, and compactness and may be useful in stopping a violent attacker. Although a .22 WMR bullet does not have the stopping power of larger-caliber bullets, sometimes just pointing a gun at an aggressor who is threatening can be effective in stopping the bad behavior. If firing is necessary for self-defense, a .22 WMR handgun may also inflict enough pain to cause the assailant to stop voluntarily. Although a .22 WMR has much less probability to bring about instant involuntary incapacitation, in some cases it may be enough to stop the aggressor.

Modular Handgun System

That the matter of stopping power versus caliber has not been completely resolved after decades of testing and operational experience with various-caliber handguns is exemplified by the US Army's Modular Handgun System program. The US Army has begun a program competition for the procurement of a handgun that is expected to replace the Beretta M9 pistol as the military's standard sidearm.

Because of concerns about the effectiveness of the 9 mm cartridge in combat zones like Iraq and Afghanistan, the US Army is having an open competition to evaluate larger rounds like the .40-caliber S&W and .45 ACP and more powerful rounds, such as the .357 SIG or FN 5.7 mm x 28 mm cartridges. In addition, expanding hollow-point bullets are not prohibited in their solicitation.

The evaluation of caliber size and muzzle energy is still ongoing today. This is not a bad thing because, politics aside, a competition is a proven method for evaluating different products and finding the best ones. After all, Glock had to do the same thing when his pistols were evaluated by the Austrian military.

As you can see ammunition evaluation as described in this chapter has been ongoing for at least a hundred years. So too has the debate among experts about which calibers have the best stopping power or the ability to incapacitate an aggressor. There is no absolute answer to this issue, and even if I were a firearms expert I would not make any claims. My purpose in reviewing the measures of effectiveness in this chapter has been to inform the reader about a complicated technical issue. Ultimately, you decide what caliber firearm to carry concealed.

Body Armor (Levels of Protection)

As body armor may be a factor in stopping a criminal assailant who is wearing it (see note below), I include here some basic information about the levels of body armor protection. Body armor may be defined as a defensive covering, generally a vest, worn to protect the body against weapons and bullets. There are four classifications of personal body armor based on the maximum level of protection provided against specific handgun threats (US DoJ NIJ 2001).

- Type I (.22 LR; .380 ACP)
- Type IIA (9 mm; .40 S&W)
- Type II (9 mm; .357 Magnum)
- Type IIIA (high-velocity 9 mm; .44 Magnum)

Body armor is also commonly described according to the materials of which it is constructed and may be (1) "soft" armor or (2) "hard" armor.

Soft armor is typically made from woven DuPont Kevlar® aramid fiber, ultrahigh-molecular-weight polyethylene, or other woven synthetic fibers. Hard armor (also called composite armor) typically consists of a front plate or insert made of a hard ceramic such as aluminum oxide, boron carbide, or silicon carbide backed up by a plastic laminate composed of fiberglass or Kevlar-reinforced plastic.

Hard or composite armor may be capable of defeating armor-piercing bullets.

Note: James Eagan Holmes, the Batman "Joker" gunman who killed people in a movie theater in Aurora, Colorado, in 2012, wore body armor.

Chapter 5

Criminal Law

I shot the sheriff, but I swear it was in self-defense.
I shot the sheriff, and they say it is a capital offense.
Eric Clapton, Song Lyrics, "I Shot the Sheriff"

Anyone who has a handgun for self-defense in the home or carries a concealed handgun must have a fundamental understanding of criminal law. As the Zimmerman trial in July 2013 demonstrated, one person's self-defense may be another person's murder. The purpose of this chapter is to define common terms used in the criminal justice system and provide some legal perspective. Chapter 5 is an alphabetical list of common terms used in criminal law that are useful to know.

Some of the legal definitions in this chapter have been reprinted from *Black's Law Dictionary* with permission of the publisher, Thomson Reuters. These definitions are identified as such by the citation (BLD) after the definition.

- assault: The threat or use of force on another that causes that person to have a reasonable apprehension of imminent harmful or offensive contact (BLD).
- aggravated assault: Criminal assault accompanied by circumstances that make it more severe, such as intent to commit another crime or the intent to cause serious bodily harm, especially by using a deadly weapon (BLD). In Utah, pointing a handgun at any part of a person's body can result in a felony charge of aggravated assault.
- assault with a deadly weapon: An aggravated assault in which the defendant, using a deadly weapon, threatens the victim with death or serious bodily injury (BLD).

- brandishing: Waving or displaying a handgun in a threatening manner or using a gun to put a person in fear of physical injury.
- capital offense: A crime for which the death penalty may be imposed; also termed *capital crime* (BLD).
- carjacking: The intentional taking of a motor vehicle belonging to another person by the use of force or intimidation.
- deadly force: Force that is likely to cause death or great bodily harm.
- dueling: The common-law offense of gunfighting at an appointed time and place after an earlier disagreement. If one is killed, the other is guilty of murder.[2]
- federal crime: A criminal offense under a federal statute. Most federal crimes are codified in Title 18 of the *United States Code* (BLD).
- federal law: The body of law consisting of the United States Constitution, federal statutes and regulations, U.S. treaties, and federal common law (BLD).
- felony: A serious crime usually punishable by imprisonment for more than one year or by death.[3]

---

2. On July 11, 1804, one of the most famous pistol duels occurred between Aaron Burr and Alexander Hamilton (the man on the ten-dollar bill). The guns used in the duel were Wogdon & Barton .56-caliber dueling pistols that had hair triggers. Burr was unscathed, but Hamilton died the next day (*Alexander Hamilton and Aaron Burr's Duel* PBS).

Dueling law in Massachusetts (chapter 265, section 3) states: "Duel; wound without and death within state. An inhabitant or resident of this commonwealth who, by previous appointment or engagement made within the same, fights a duel outside of its jurisdiction, and in so doing inflicts a mortal wound upon a person whereof he dies within the commonwealth shall be guilty of murder within the commonwealth and may be indicted, tried and convicted in the county where the death occurs."

3. Florida Statute 776.08 defines "forcible felony" as "treason; murder; manslaughter; sexual battery; carjacking; home-invasion robbery; robbery; burglary; arson; kidnapping; aggravated assault; aggravated battery; aggravated stalking; aircraft piracy; unlawful throwing, placing, or discharging of a destructive device or bomb; and any other felony

- Fifth Amendment: The amendment to the U.S. Constitution, ratified with the Bill of Rights in 1791, providing that no person shall be compelled in any criminal case to be a witness against himself (herself). A person exercising this right is sometimes referred to as "taking the Fifth." It is also known as the right against self-incrimination (see *Miranda rule*). Depending upon the circumstances, a shooter in a self-defense situation may be wise to assert this right when questioned by law enforcement officials after a shooting.
- firearm and ballistics examination: A branch of forensic science focused on the examination of bullets, cartridge cases, and firearms left at the scene of a shooting, or trying to match a bullet fired to a specific gun to solve a crime (e.g., murder weapon).
- forensic: Relating to the use of science and technology to investigate and establish facts in a court of law.
- forensic evidence: Evidence used in court; especially evidence obtained by scientific or technical means, such as ballistic or medical evidence (BLD).
- forensic science: Although this term comprises a broad range of disciplines that have their own distinct methods, the specific discipline within forensic science that involves bullets and handguns is called firearms examination or forensic ballistics.
- fugitive from justice: A criminal suspect or witness in a criminal case who flees, evades, or escapes arrest, prosecution, imprisonment, service of process, or the giving of testimony, especially by fleeing the jurisdiction or by hiding. See 18 U.S.C.A. § 1073 (BLD).
- homicide: The killing of one person by another. The legal term for killing a man or a woman, whether lawfully or unlawfully. See *justifiable homicide*.

---

which involves the use or threat of physical force or violence against any individual."

- ignorance: Ignorance of the law is no excuse. Not knowing the law is not a legitimate defense in any firearm or self-defense case.
- imminent danger: An immediate, real threat to one's safety that justifies the use of force in self-defense (BLD).
- intent: The state of mind operative at the time of an action.
- justifiable homicide: The killing of another in self-defense when faced with the danger of death or serious bodily injury. Also termed *excusable homicide* (BLD).
- manslaughter: The unlawful killing of a human being without malice aforethought (BLD).
    - involuntary manslaughter: Homicide in which there is no intention to kill or do grievous bodily harm, but that is committed with criminal negligence or during the commission of a crime (BLD).
    - voluntary manslaughter: An act of murder reduced to manslaughter because of extenuating circumstances, such as adequate provocation (BLD).[4]
- Miranda rule (1966): In criminal law, Miranda is the legal doctrine that a criminal suspect in police custody must be informed of certain constitutional rights before being interrogated (i.e., the Fifth Amendment right against self-incrimination). The suspect must be advised of the right to remain silent, the right to have an attorney present during questioning, and the right to have an attorney appointed if the suspect cannot afford one. If a suspect is not advised of these rights or does not validly waive them, any evidence obtained during the interrogation cannot be used against the suspect at trial

---

4. The term "voluntary" implies the exercise of free will or choice. Voluntary manslaughter is deliberate or intentional and is done on purpose. Involuntary manslaughter means the act was not done willingly or on purpose or was not subject to control.

[*Miranda v. Arizona*, 384 U.S. 436, 86 S.Ct. 1602 (1966)]. Also often called Miranda warning.

- misdemeanor: A crime that is less serious than a felony and is usually punishable by fine, penalty, forfeiture, or confinement in a jail.
- murder: The killing of a human being with malice aforethought. Malice aforethought is the requisite mental state for common-law murder, encompassing any one of the following: (1) intent to kill, (2) the intent to inflict grievous bodily harm, (3) extremely reckless indifference to the value of human life, or (4) the intent to commit a dangerous felony (BLD).
  - first-degree murder: Murder that is willful, deliberate, or premeditated, or that is committed during the course of another dangerous felony. Murder by poisoning or by lying in wait is considered first-degree murder (BLD).
  - second-degree murder: Murder that is not aggravated by any of the circumstances of first-degree murder. All types of murder not involving willful, deliberate, and premeditated killing are usually considered second-degree murder (BLD).[5]
- pistol-whipping: An act of using a handgun as a blunt weapon to strike a person in the head.
- Second Amendment: See chapter 7, "Self-Defense Laws."
- self-defense: Use of force to protect oneself or one's family from a real or threatened attack. Generally, a person is justified in using deadly force in self-defense or in defense of another *only if* defending against another's deadly force or threat of serious bodily harm.

---

5. In his widely covered criminal trial in Florida in 2013, George Zimmerman was charged with second-degree murder and claimed self-defense.

In his book *The Law of Self-Defense*, Andrew F. Branca (attorney at law) identifies five legal principles of self-defense that are necessary to justify self-defense:

- Innocence. Legitimate self-defense is only justified if you are an innocent party and did not initiate, sustain, or escalate the confrontation.
- Imminence. An attack must be about to occur so quickly that it cannot be avoided safely in order to establish self-defense as justified.
- Proportionality. The force you use in self-defense cannot be greater than the force you are threatened with.
- Avoidance. In certain states and under specific circumstances, one might be required by law to retreat to avoid a conflict.
- Reasonableness. Use of force cannot be justified as self-defense unless your actions are perceived to be subjectively and objectively reasonable.

Mr. Branca's book is a comprehensive legal description of the principles of self-defense that must be met in a court of law in a self-defense case. I highly recommend it for further reading to better understand the legal concepts of self-defense.

- statute: A law passed by a legislative body (BLD). It is important to know all the state statutes relating to concealed carry and self-defense where you intend to carry a concealed handgun.
- straw purchase: A transaction where one person purchases a firearm on behalf of an undisclosed person. A straw purchase might be legal or illegal, depending upon the circumstances. Maryland Senate Bill 281

(Firearm Safety Act of 2013) defines "straw purchase" as follows:

> Straw purchase means a sale of a regulated firearm in which a person uses another, known as the straw purchaser to:
>
> - complete the application to purchase a regulated firearm;
> - take initial possession of the regulated firearm; and
> - subsequently, transfer the regulated firearm to the person.

- U.S.C.: Acronym for *United States Code*, the official name for US federal laws. Federal laws, which are also known as federal statutes, are organized into a set of fifty numbered "titles" that make up the *United States Code*. The most important federal gun laws are contained under Title 18, "Crimes and Criminal Procedures." Federal laws within the *US Code* are designated by a numbering system that identifies the title, section, subsection, paragraph, and subparagraph. For example, the citation 18 U.S.C. § 922 (v & w) means Title 18 of the *United States Code*, section 922, subsections (v) and (w).
- U.S.C.A.: Acronym for *United States Code Annotated*. The *US Code Annotated* is a multivolume publication of the complete text of the *United States Code* with historical notes, cross-references, and case notes of federal and state decisions construing specific code sections (BLD).

The next chapter addresses various concealed-carry laws and restrictions that may be helpful to know to stay within the confines of the law.

Chapter 6

Concealed-Carry Laws

*The Second Amendment of our Bill of
Rights is my concealed weapons permit, period.*
Ted Nugent

Not Quite. Read On.
Author

Chapter 6 describes the license-to-carry permit process for concealed carry in the United States, restrictions on concealed carry, and some laws intended to protect firearms owners. Some specific examples of handgun violations are recounted to make the point that a concealed-carry holder must at all times be aware of pertinent laws and the restrictions placed upon them. If one is not aware of concealed-carry restrictions, it is very easy to make a serious mistake that may result in criminal charges and jail time.

Concealed Carry (Definition)

The Florida Legislature defines a concealed firearm as any firearm "carried on or about a person in such a manner as to conceal it from the ordinary sight of another person." A person carrying a concealed firearm in Florida without a license is guilty of a felony of the third degree. The penalty for this offense is a prison term of up to five years. Florida's statutes clearly state that a license to carry is essential to avoid committing a felony if you wish to carry a loaded handgun on your person.

Suggested reading:

Your resident state statutes pertaining to the concealed carry of firearms.

Non-resident state statutes of those states where you plan to carry concealed.

Government Accountability Office. 2012, July. *Gun Control: States' Laws and Requirements for Concealed Carry Permits Vary across the Nation.* GAO-12-717.

License to Carry (LTC)

The term *license to carry* refers to the permits issued by various states that authorize individuals to carry concealed handguns legally in their respective states. Other terms used by states for concealed carry licenses/permits for handguns include: carry concealed weapon (CCW), concealed carry license (CCL), concealed carry permit (CCP), concealed firearm permit (CFP), concealed handgun permit (CHP), concealed pistol license (CPL), concealed weapon permit (CWP), and weapons carry license (WCL). In this book I use LTC and CCW interchangeably to mean the same thing and to include these other names.

Fifty States

Laws regulating concealed carry of firearms vary from state-to-state. States may be classified into one of the following three categories based on their concealed-carry laws:

1. Shall issue
2. May issue
3. Permit not required

Concealed-Carry Laws

Shall issue refers to the statutory language in a state where the issuance of a license to carry (LTC) concealed weapons is *not* dependent upon the discretion of a law enforcement officer. In a shall-issue state, if an applicant meets specific objective criteria, has no disqualifying criminal record, and completes whatever training is required by law, the applicant *must* be issued a license regardless of what the issuing authority personally thinks of the individual.

May issue refers to states that allow local law enforcement officers a certain amount of discretion over the issuance of an LTC permit. Even though an applicant may meet specific defined criteria, a local official may deny the applicant a license based on other subjective criteria. These states are also commonly referred to as *discretionary issue* states.

Permit not required refers to a state where no permit is required to carry a concealed handgun in that state. There are eight such states: Alaska, Arizona, Kansas, Maine, Montana, Vermont, West Virginia, and Wyoming (Hawkins 2016).

All fifty of the United States allow state residents to carry concealed handguns if specific criteria are met. Most states also issue permits to nonresidents if they are eligible. The GAO report cited above in this chapter describes the number and kinds of LTC permits issued in the United States. Up until June 2013, there had been one remaining no-issue state that did not allow any resident citizen to carry a concealed handgun. Illinois was the last no-issue state, but that was changed with legislation permitting concealed carry.

In an attempt to legalize concealed carry across all fifty states using one's resident LTC permit, on April 17, 2013, US Senator John Cornyn (R-TX) proposed the Constitutional Concealed Carry Reciprocity Act. This Act would have allowed concealed-carry permits in one state to be valid in all the other states (just like driver's licenses). Sixty votes were needed to pass the bill, which fell short in the US Senate by three votes, fifty-seven to forty-three. More recent attempts have been tried but the votes are not there yet.

District of Columbia

Prior to July 24, 2014 the federal District of Columbia prohibited carrying concealed handguns altogether. You could not bear arms in Washington, DC, outside of your home. Even possession of unregistered ammunition was illegal in the District of Columbia.

Suggested reading:

Miller, Emily. 2013. *Emily Gets Her Gun...But Obama Wants to Take Yours*. Washington, DC: Regnery.

On July 24, 2014, U.S District Judge Frederick J. Scullin ruled in a decision concerning the carrying of handguns for self-defense, that the current ban in the District of Columbia violates the US Constitution. In his decision he stated:

> In light of *Heller, McDonald*, and their progeny, there is no longer any basis on which this court can conclude that the District of Columbia's total ban on the public carrying of ready-to-use handguns outside the house is constitutional under any level of scrutiny. Therefore, the Court finds that the District of Columbia's complete ban on carrying of handguns in public is unconstitutional.

The *Heller* and *McDonald* US Supreme Court cases are discussed in chapter 7. The D.C. case quoted above is a major positive step forward for concealed carry in the District of Columbia. It establishes that D.C.'s ban on concealed carry by residents was unconstitutional and cannot be enforced any longer. However, it would be very prudent to check with D.C. authorities pertaining to concealed carry of firearms before doing so. If there are pending court cases that are still unresolved and law enforcement is not in compliance, there is still potential jeopardy if you carry in D.C. I do not know what the concealed-carry law is regarding non-residents.

Suggested reading:

US District Court, *Tom G. Palmer et al. v. District of Columbia and Cathy Lanier*. Memorandum-Decision and Order, July 24, 2014. Frederick J. Scullin Jr., Senior US District Court Judge.

Nonresident CCW or Pistol Permits

Most states allow nonresidents from other states to apply for a pistol permit to allow concealed carry of handguns in their states in accordance with their laws. In some states such a permit is referred to as a CCW permit (i.e., carrying a concealed weapon). The qualification criteria are generally very similar from state to state.

Each state generally requires proof of age, a criminal record check for misdemeanors or felonies, a current photo, and proof that the applicant has taken a firearms safety course. Some states also require fingerprints. Each application inquires about drug offenses and whether the applicant has been treated for a mental illness or disorder or is a fugitive from justice.

Assuming an applicant is granted a pistol permit, each state has its own statutes that place restrictions on concealed carry, although these restrictions are also generally very similar from state to state. Listed below in Table 17 are five states from which the author has obtained applications for comparison purposes:

Table 17. Cost of Selected Non-Resident Handgun Permits

State	Fee	Term of License
Connecticut	$67	5 years
Florida	$112	7 years
Maine	$60	4 years
Massachusetts	$150	1 year
New Hampshire	$100	4 years

(As of 2014)

The major differences between the states' permits are in the terms of the licenses and the fees, which include the applicant's additional costs associated with processing, fingerprinting, criminal record checks (state and local), and mailing costs. Massachusetts nonresident pistol permits cost approximately $150 ($100 for the application and $50 for associated costs). The Massachusetts license is only valid for *one year* and requires a complete resubmittal of all previously submitted papers with a new fingerprint and photo *each year*.

With the application forms, I received in the mail a copy of all applicable state gun laws from Florida (twenty-six pages), Connecticut (four pages), and Maine (sixteen pages). A close comparison of the selected state gun laws reveals that they are indeed fundamentally very similar, and a case can be made that CCW permits in one state are just about the same in any other state. This would seem to justify the US Senate's attempt at passing a Constitutional Concealed Carry Reciprocity Act that would allow concealed-carry permits in one state to be valid in all the other states (just like driver's licenses).

In absence of such a law, the law-abiding citizen has an extremely time-consuming and costly process to obtain nonresident state gun permits. On the other hand, it seems unlikely that a fugitive from justice or a felon will obtain a gun permit application to apply in accordance with the law. And if so, how many fugitives from justice are going to admit to that on the form?

New York is one state that deserves particular attention. According to the New York State Police, New York does not issue permits for concealed carry to nonresidents. This means that nonresidents of New York are not legally allowed to carry a concealed firearm in New York, unless I suppose there are exceptions or exemptions which I was not informed about. The letter I received simply stated that New York State does not issue non-resident concealed-carry licenses.

One Tennessee woman found out the hard way what happens when you carry a concealed handgun into New York, even if it is legal and you are licensed to carry in the state where you live. Meredith Graves was visiting the 9/11 Memorial in New York City in 2011 when she tried to check her handgun with police after seeing a sign prohibiting guns. She was arrested and charged with felony criminal possession of a firearm. She had not realized that her gun permit was not valid in New York. Her charge was eventually plea-bargained to misdemeanor possession without jail time (Grace 2012). The lesson here is that you need to know the concealed-carry laws of the state you are visiting. You can get into a lot of trouble not knowing the law, even if you have good intentions.

Another high-profile handgun case in New York was that of Plaxico Burress, a former New York Giants football superstar. Burress was at a nightclub in Manhattan in November 2008 when a gun that was tucked in his waistband slipped down his leg and fired, shooting him in the right thigh. The bullet narrowly missed a nightclub security guard standing inches away. It lodged in the floor and was recovered by a bartender.

The handgun was not licensed in New York or in New Jersey, where Burress lived. His license to carry a concealed weapon in the state of Florida had expired in May 2008 and was not relevant in New York anyway. Burress was convicted of a firearms crime and served nearly two years in prison (*ESPN News*, Sept 23, 2009.)

Concealed-Carry Restrictions

Once you have been issued a license-to-carry firearms permit in a given state you need to be aware of locations where the concealed carry of firearms is still prohibited, even though you have a permit. These locations are referred to as no-carry places. Entering a location with a firearm where it is prohibited can result in fines and/or imprisonment. Some states will send you a copy of the applicable laws with your permit and a list of prohibited places. Other states do not send this information leaving it up to you to find out. I summarize below various no-carry locations, some other concealed-carry restrictions, and provide some other examples of people who violated the law and got in trouble.

No-Carry Places

Concealed-carry licenses do not permit individuals to carry concealed handguns everywhere. Many states' gun laws prohibit carrying concealed weapons into such places as elementary schools, colleges, and universities; bars and restaurants that serve alcohol; courthouses; places of worship; detention facilities, prisons, and jails; government buildings; polling places; and so on. Federal law prohibits the carry of concealed weapons in federal facilities, which includes federal buildings, post offices, military bases, and airports. These places are referred to as no-carry places.

For example, in Florida the Jack Hagler Self-Defense Act (section 790.06 of Florida Statutes) lists several places you may *not* carry a concealed handgun even if you have a concealed-carry permit. In Florida you cannot carry a concealed handgun into police stations, prisons or jails, courthouses or courtrooms, polling places, public schools (elementary and secondary), bars or other establishments where alcohol is consumed, at any school, college or professional athletic event, colleges and universities, and airports.

In Texas, Concealed Carry Handgun Law (2011–2012) section 46.035, Unlawful Carrying of Handgun by License Holder, prohibits concealed carry of a handgun on the premises of a business where consumption of alcohol constitutes 51 percent or more of its income from the sale of alcoholic beverages; where a high school, collegiate, or professional sporting event or interscholastic event is taking place; at a correctional facility; at a licensed hospital or nursing home; at an amusement park; in a church, synagogue, or other place of worship; or at any meeting of a government entity.[6]

These two examples demonstrate that it would be extremely time consuming and futile to try to summarize concealed-carry handgun laws of all fifty states and territories here, or note no-carry exceptions for every kind of property or establishment where you may find yourself. Even if I did, that information might be out of date before this book could make it to the reader. But the examples given in this chapter should serve as a compelling argument to the reader that you should read up on the carry laws for the jurisdiction where you will be *before* you get there—not after you're already in trouble.

---

6. The "51 percent" provision has me perplexed. How in the hell is a concealed-carry holder supposed to know whether an establishment that serves both food and alcoholic beverages receives 51 percent or more of its income from the sale of its alcoholic beverages? You would have to know this before entering an establishment, or you could be breaking the law. Are you supposed to write a letter to the company and ask about its business income before going there? Good luck with that.

Federal Facilities

Federal law prohibits the possession and concealed carry of firearms and dangerous weapons in federal facilities, except by law enforcement personnel performing their official duties. This includes all federal government buildings and federal court facilities (18 U.S.C. § 930). Post office buildings and military installations anywhere, federal prisons, and buildings leased by the federal government are all places where it is illegal to carry a concealed handgun. One little unknowing slipup or inattentive moment on your part could make you a criminal (e.g., not thinking when going into a post office to buy stamps while you are carrying a concealed pistol is a crime).

Example 1: *Violation in Maine*. After walking past five signs warning people not to bring firearms into the building, a man in Maine brought a loaded handgun into a Veterans Affairs community-based outpatient clinic to show an employee his "newest baby." He was told that he could not bring a gun into the building or onto the property. Three days later, the man returned and was patted down by an officer, whom he told that he left his gun in his car. The officer went to the man's car and found a Kimber .45-caliber semiautomatic pistol under a shirt on the front passenger seat. It was loaded with seven rounds of .45-caliber hollow-point ammunition. The man was charged with two firearms violations. In a plea agreement, the charge relating to showing the gun to an employee was dismissed. Regarding the second charge, he pleaded guilty to carrying a firearm onto federal property and was fined $1,000 (*Bangor Daily News*, August 7, 2013).

There are several lessons that a responsible concealed-carry holder can learn from this incident. First, one must know what constitutes federal property. In this case, federal property was not just the building but also the parking lot. Two,

86

ignoring signs prohibiting firearms in a building is just plain stupid. Three, leaving a loaded gun on the seat of a car is irresponsible and in some jurisdictions is another firearms violation. Fourth, assuming the man had a concealed-carry license, it could be subject to revocation. Fifth, if he did not have a license that would constitute another firearms violation, probably a felony.

Example 2: *District of Columbia (Jack Ruby's gun)*. In 1992 a man named Robert Luongo carried the handgun that Jack Ruby used in 1963 to kill Lee Harvey Oswald to Capitol Hill while sightseeing, only to have the gun, then worth $220,000, seized by the US Capitol Police. Ruby bought the .38-caliber Colt Cobra in a Dallas pawnshop for seventy-five dollars in 1961. In 1992 and still today, in the District of Columbia one cannot possess a handgun unless it is registered.

Luongo was charged with carrying a gun without a license and with possessing an unregistered handgun. He said that he was unaware that the District's guns laws required carrying permits even for historic, unloaded guns (Mooar 1992). The lesson learned from this incident is that there are no exceptions to carrying a handgun on federal property, even if you are carrying a historic, unloaded, valuable gun and have good intentions. Luongo was in town to show the gun on the *Larry King Live* TV show.

For more on the outrageous handgun laws and procedures that still exist in Washington, DC, even after the *Heller* decision, read *Emily Gets Her Gun* by Emily Miller.

Airline Travel

The Transportation Security Administration (TSA) prohibits the transport of firearms and ammunition in carry-on baggage. Airline travelers may only transport *unloaded* firearms in a locked, hard-sided container as checked baggage. For more information, go to http://www.tsa.gov/traveler-information/firearms-and-ammunition.[7]

Brandishing

Waving or displaying a handgun in a threatening manner or using a gun to put a person in reasonable fear of imminent physical injury is brandishing a firearm. Brandishing a handgun is a serious misdemeanor that can result in the loss of a person's concealed-carry permit.

Example 1: *Brandishing Law in Maine*. In Maine, a person (even one with a permit to carry concealed) may not display a firearm in a threatening manner (Title 25 Maine Revised Statutes Annotated [MRSA] § 2001).

Example 2: *Brandishing Law in Virginia*. In Virginia, it is unlawful to point, hold, or brandish any firearm in such a manner as to induce fear in the mind of another of being shot or injured, unless the person with the firearm is engaged in self-defense (Virginia Law § 18.2-282, Pointing, holding, or brandishing firearm).

Drinking and Drugs

A basic gun safety rule is to never use firearms while under the influence of alcohol or drugs. In general, states have criminal laws that make it a crime to use a firearm while under the influence of alcohol or drugs.

---

7. In the first six months of 2013, TSA screeners found 894 guns on passengers or in their carry-on bags. That was a 30 percent increase over the same period the previous year. In 2012, TSA found 1,549 firearms on passengers attempting to go through screeners. That was a 17 percent increase from 2011. TSA cannot explain why so many passengers are still trying to board planes with handguns (Joan Lowy, "More Airline Passengers Showing Up with Guns," Associated Press, *Greenfield Recorder*, July 3, 2013).

For example, Connecticut's law reads as follows:

> Sec. 53-206d. Carrying of firearm while under the influence of intoxicating liquor or drug prohibited. Class B misdemeanor. (a) No person shall carry a pistol, a revolver, a machine gun, shotgun, rifle or other firearm, which is loaded and from which a shot may be discharged, upon his person (1) while under the influence of intoxicating liquor or any drug or both or (2) while the ratio of alcohol in the blood of such person is ten-hundredths of one percent (0.10 percent) or more of alcohol by weight.[8]

Premises Where Alcohol Is Sold and Consumed

If you are a person who likes to have an alcoholic beverage with a meal in a restaurant, you may find the guns laws relating to concealed carry of a handgun and consumption of alcohol a little difficult to understand. The laws vary widely from state to state, and some are ambiguous. This is one of those areas where concealed-carry holders should carefully research the laws of the applicable states where they intend to be.

---

8. This law is ambiguous. The first part implies it is illegal to carry a firearm if one has drunk any amount of alcohol, since one or two drinks can influence a person's behavior; the second part implies it is only illegal if one is intoxicated as defined by a blood alcohol concentration of 0.10 percent or greater. My recommendation would be not to drink anything before and while carrying a firearm and to follow the basic safety rules.

Montana is an example of a state that prohibits the concealed carry of a weapon in a "room" where alcohol is consumed. This would include restaurants that serve alcoholic beverages. The Montana law reads as follows:

> State of Montana 45-8-328. Carrying concealed weapon in prohibited place—penalty. (1) Except for legislative security officers authorized to carry a concealed weapon in the state capitol as provided in 45-8-317(1)(k), a person commits the offense of carrying a concealed weapon in a prohibited place if the person purposely or knowingly carries a concealed weapon in:
>
> (c) a room in which alcoholic beverages are sold, dispensed, and consumed under a license issued under Title 16 for the sale of alcoholic beverages for consumption on the premises.
>
> (2) It is not a defense that the person had a valid permit to carry a concealed weapon. A person convicted of the offense shall be imprisoned in the county jail for a term not to exceed 6 months or fined an amount not to exceed $500, or both.

The Montana law example shows that in that state, a valid concealed-carry license will still not permit you to carry in a restaurant that serves alcohol.

The good news for concealed-carry holders is that most states allow concealed-carry license holders to eat in dining areas of restaurants that serve alcohol, unless otherwise posted. However, at least seven states (Illinois, Louisiana, Montana, North and South Carolina, North Dakota, and Texas) either prohibit or qualify concealed carry in restaurants.

Driving State to State

Concealed carry while driving a vehicle from state to state requires a major effort by a gun owner. For example, in New England where several states are close together, persons wishing to exercise their Second Amendment right to carry a concealed handgun for self-defense purposes while driving a car through neighboring states must have a valid pistol permit for each of those states (except Vermont). Consider the problem to be analogous to needing a driver's license for each state you drive in.

With respect to concealed carry of handguns, a resident of Massachusetts must have a valid resident license-to-carry permit, and typically would also need a nonresident permit for New Hampshire, Connecticut, Maine, and Rhode Island. Vermont does not require a pistol permit for concealed carry. New York does not issue nonresident permits. The time and cost involved in getting these permits is substantial. That is why a national Constitutional Concealed Carry Reciprocity Act makes so much sense and would enable US citizens to exercise their Second Amendment right without infringement.

Another reason for this law is because just driving from one state to another can turn a law-abiding gun owner in their home state into a felon if convicted in a state where their gun permit is not valid. The example below is a case in point.

Example: In 2014 a mother of two children from Philadelphia faced two felony counts for transporting her legally owned gun into New Jersey. Shaneen Allen possessed a concealed-carry permit from her home state of Pennsylvania but did not know that her permit was not valid in New Jersey. She was stopped by police for a minor traffic violation. She informed the officer that she had a gun permit and was carrying a concealed weapon (something recommended by many experts). She faced felony charges of illegal possession of a firearm and hollow-point bullets. Illegal possession of the handgun is punishable by a minimum mandatory three years in prison (Cruz and Miller 2014).

One has to wonder why hollow-point bullets are illegal in New Jersey, because these bullets are the preferred ammunition for concealed carry just about everywhere else for sound reasons, including public safety.

School Zones

As cited in more detail in chapter 8, there is federal law that makes it unlawful for any individual to possess a firearm in a school zone. The term *school zone* in general includes elementary or secondary schools and colleges and universities. However, the federal law allows for an exception if the individual possessing the firearm is licensed to carry by the state in question.

Example: Under its general laws, Massachusetts prohibits the carrying of concealed handguns in school zones even if one has a concealed carry permit.

> *MGL Chapter 269, Crimes against Public Peace, section 10(j) Carrying dangerous weapons).* (j) For the purposes of this paragraph, "firearm" shall mean any pistol, revolver, rifle or smoothbore arm from which a shot, bullet or pellet can be discharged.

> Whoever, not being a law enforcement officer and notwithstanding any license obtained by the person pursuant to chapter 140, carries on the person a firearm, loaded or unloaded, or other dangerous weapon in any building or on the grounds of any elementary or secondary school,

college or university without the written authorization of the board or officer in charge of the elementary or secondary school, college or university shall be punished by a fine of not more than $1,000 or by imprisonment for not more than 2 years or both. A law enforcement officer may arrest without a warrant and detain a person found carrying a firearm in violation of this paragraph.

Any officer in charge of an elementary or secondary school, college or university or any faculty member or administrative officer of an elementary or secondary school, college or university that fails to report a violation of this paragraph shall be guilty of a misdemeanor and punished by a fine of not more than $500.

Policies prohibiting the carrying of concealed handguns in school zones may need to be reconsidered in light of the recent FBI report discussed in chapter 1. Given the short time intervals of school shootings, teachers who are enabled and voluntarily carry a concealed handgun may be in the best position to stop crazed shooters on school grounds.

College Campuses

Carrying concealed handguns on college campuses is prohibited in most states. However, there is a growing trend to allow concealed carry of handguns at colleges and universities. In 2006 Utah became the first state to allow concealed carry on campus. In 2014 Idaho became the seventh state to allow "campus carry" despite opposition by many students, faculty, and college administrators. The seven states that permit concealed carry on campus as of this writing are Colorado, Idaho, Kansas, Mississippi, Oregon, Utah, and Wisconsin. Colleges may still impose carry restrictions in certain buildings and rooms or at specific events (Millward and Forman 2014).

Example: The Colorado Legislative Council Staff issued a memorandum, dated August 14, 2012, addressing concealed carry at public colleges and universities. The relevant part of that memo is as follows:

The Colorado Supreme Court ruled in 2012 that a University of Colorado system wide ban on concealed handguns overstepped the university regents' authority. As such, the university and 30 other public institutions of higher learning in the state are required to allow the carrying of concealed handguns by valid permit holders.

Banks and Financial Institutions

Let's say you have a valid concealed-carry permit in your state of residence. You are driving your car with a concealed handgun on your person, and you decide that you need to stop at your savings bank to conduct some banking business. Is it legal for you to enter your bank carrying your concealed handgun? The answer to that simple question is rather complicated and depends upon the state, town, and bank where you are at.

Before I attempt to answer that question, let me offer a caveat. Again it is up to you, the reader, to determine the legality in the state, town, and bank regarding concealed carry. Here I provide an example to demonstrate the variation between states and the limitations or exceptions that may apply.

Example: Montana is a state that prohibits any person (who has a gun permit or not) from carrying a concealed weapon into a bank, credit union, savings and loan institution, or similar business (i.e., financial institutions).

The applicable Montana statute is as follows:

> State of Montana 45-8-328. Carrying concealed weapon in prohibited place—penalty. (1) Except for legislative security officers authorized to carry a concealed weapon in the state capitol as provided in 45-8-317(1)(k), a person commits the offense of carrying a concealed weapon in a prohibited place if the person purposely or knowingly carries a concealed weapon in...
>
> (b) a bank, credit union, savings and loan institution, or similar institution during the institution's normal business hours. It is not an offense under this section to carry a concealed weapon while:
>
> (i) using an institution's drive-up window, automatic teller machine, or unstaffed night depository; or
>
> (ii) at or near a branch office of an institution in a mall, grocery store, or other place unless the person is inside the enclosure used for the institution's financial services or is using the institution's financial services.
>
> (2) It is not a defense that the person had a valid permit to carry a concealed weapon. A person convicted of the offense shall be imprisoned in the county jail for a term not to exceed 6 months or fined an amount not to exceed $500, or both.

From examining this statute, you can get a sense of the ambiguity that may exist in such a law, the fine line that exists between committing and not committing a crime, and the difficulty a law-abiding citizen may have in trying to comply with the law. Section (b) seems pretty clear. It states that you cannot carry a concealed handgun in a bank. Section 2 is also pretty clear. Having a valid concealed-carry permit is not an exception. Furthermore, Section b (i) lists three exceptions that at first glance seem pretty clear too. You can use a drive-up window, an ATM, or an unstaffed night depository while carrying a concealed handgun.

The ATM is the one I have difficulty with. My bank has two ATMs. One is a drive-up, and the other is a walk-in ATM at the entrance of the bank. What if the ATM is located inside the bank's building enclosure like it is at my bank? If you walk ten feet from the indoor ATM, you will be in the bank where financial services are taking place. But the indoor ATM is still under the bank's roof (i.e., enclosure). My interpretation of the Montana law (if it were to apply to me in my state) is that carrying a concealed handgun to an outdoor drive-up ATM is legal, but carrying to an indoor ATM is not. If I used the walk-in ATM instead of the drive-up ATM, I would be committing a crime.

Reciprocity

By definition, reciprocity implies a mutual cooperative arrangement of privileges (i.e., a two-way agreement). With respect to concealed-carry permits, some states have reciprocity agreements with other states, which means each state honors the concealed-carry permits of the other. However, some states may recognize the concealed-carry permit of another state, but the reverse is not true. This is not reciprocity if it works only one way. For example, Texas recognizes a concealed-carry permit from Massachusetts, while Massachusetts does not honor a concealed-carry permit from Texas. Such an arrangement is one-way only and is more appropriately referred to as recognition by Texas. There is no reciprocity with Massachusetts. See also *permit recognition.*

Permit Recognition

Permit recognition is a term given to a law that allows a person to carry a firearm within a state if he/she has a carry permit issued by another state, and such permit meets the requirements of the state in which the firearm is carried.

Many concealed-carry advocates highly recommend a Utah nonresident CCW permit because it enables an individual to carry a concealed handgun in thirty-one states: Alabama, Alaska, Arizona, Arkansas, Delaware, Georgia, Indiana, Idaho, Iowa, Kentucky, Louisiana, Minnesota, Missouri, Mississippi, Montana, Nebraska, North Carolina, North Dakota, Ohio, Oklahoma, Pennsylvania, South Dakota, Tennessee, Texas, Utah, Virginia, Vermont, Washington, West Virginia, Wisconsin, and Wyoming. That being said, this author is still hopeful for the ideal solution, which would be the US Congress passing a bill that would allow concealed-carry permits in one state to be valid in all the other states (just like driver's licenses).

Firearms Owners' Private Information

On April 17, 2013, US Senator John Barrasso (R-WY), successfully included an amendment to the Safe Communities, Safe Schools Act (S. 649) that protects law-abiding gun owners across the nation from having their private gun ownership information released to the public. The amendment passed the Senate by a vote of sixty-seven to thirty. Barrasso's amendment number 717 withholds program funding if a state or local government publicly releases information on individuals who have licenses to purchase, possess, or carry firearms.

This issue came to light nationwide in 2012 when a New York newspaper (the *Journal News*) mapped out online the names and addresses of pistol permit holders in Westchester and Rockland counties in New York. The newspaper received a wave of criticism for doing so because many people believe that this information can be used by criminals to identify homes where guns could be stolen, or to identify homeowners who are unprotected and more vulnerable to robbery and other serious crimes. The federal law passed by the Senate will basically punish states that allow publication of firearms owners' private information.

Firearms Owners' Protection Act (FOPA)

The FOPA of 1986 (18 U.S.C. § 926A) is a US law that revised much of the Gun Control Act of 1968. One of the key sections of FOPA (known as the "safe passage" provision) regulates the interstate transportation of firearms and is particularly important to handgun owners. The safe passage provision protects persons traveling from one state to another from being incarcerated for a firearms offense in a state that has strict gun control laws, if the traveler is just passing through (e.g., stopping for fuel, food, or overnight hotel), and provided that the firearms and ammunition are not immediately accessible, that the firearms are unloaded, and in the case of a vehicle without a compartment separate from the driver's compartment, the firearms are located in a locked container. This provision protects the rights of gun owners to legally transport their firearms between locations where they are legally allowed to possess them. See also chapter 8, the section on "Interstate Transportation of Firearms."[9]

Example: In 2013 a man from Brattleboro, Vermont, was arrested on multiple firearms charges after being stopped in Whately, Massachusetts, for an expired car registration. A pretow search of his car revealed a loaded

---

9. It is important to understand this provision does not allow a gun owner to carry a concealed handgun from state to state. The firearms transported must be unloaded and locked up. Only a state permit will allow concealed carry of a loaded handgun through that state.

9 mm pistol in a holster under the driver's seat. The van's cargo area also contained an unloaded TEC-9 pistol with a pair of empty thirty-round magazines, well over the state's ten-round limit. Also found were a .308-caliber semiautomatic rifle, a matching twenty-round magazine loaded with nineteen rounds, and another empty twenty-round magazine, as well as cartridges in a plastic bag and several open boxes of ammunition totaling more than 150 rounds.

The man was arrested and charged with carrying a firearm without a license and two counts of possession of a firearm without a firearm identification card. The weapons, magazines, and ammunition found were legal in the man's home state of Vermont. Vermont doesn't require a license or permit to possess or carry loaded firearms, only that purchasers pass an in-store background check.

Because the firearms were not unloaded and not locked up, the driver was not in compliance with the laws that allow firearms to be transported through Massachusetts without an in-state license. Had the weapons been unloaded and locked up, FOPA could have protected the man from arrest and most of the firearms charges. He still may have been charged with possession of magazines that exceeded the Massachusetts magazine limit of ten. This case is illustrative of the major difference in gun laws that may exist between bordering states (in this case, Vermont and Massachusetts) and why it is so important to know applicable state and federal laws (Greenfield Recorder 2013).

Registration of Firearms

Registration of firearms refers to a list, record, or registry of firearms legally owned by law-abiding owners maintained by a state or federal agency. Federal statutes do not prohibit states from requiring gun owners to register their firearms. Most states do *not* require the registration of handguns. Some do. Hawaii has a very comprehensive registration system, requiring all firearms, with minor exceptions, to be registered. The District of Columbia also requires firearm registration.

Some states have laws prohibiting the registration of firearms. For example, the State of Florida prohibits the registration of firearms because it can "become an instrument for profiling, harassing, or abusing law-abiding citizens based on their choice to own a firearm and exercise their Second Amendment right to keep and bear arms as guaranteed under the US Constitution. Further, such a list, record, or registry has the potential to fall into the wrong hands and become a shopping list for thieves" (Florida Statute 790.335, Prohibition of Registration of Firearms).

As Judge Napolitano notes:

> Some would argue that registration and licensing weapons are not really infringements [of the Second Amendment], but would anyone seriously argue that citizens must register with the police and obtain a license in order to exercise freely their political or religious [First Amendment] beliefs? (Napolitano 2010)

Chapter 7

Self-Defense Laws

Laws that forbid the carrying of arms...disarm only those who are neither inclined nor determined to commit crimes...Such laws make things worse for the assaulted and better for the assailants; they serve rather to encourage than to prevent homicides, for an unarmed man may be attacked with greater confidence than an armed man.
Thomas Jefferson's *Commonplace Book*, 1774–1776, quoting from *On Crimes and Punishment*, by criminologist Cesare Beccaria, 1764

Chapter 7 describes various legal concepts that relate to the use of handguns in a self-defense situation. These legal concepts are very important because they relate to the use of deadly force and may determine whether a person is justified for killing someone in self-defense or will be guilty of and convicted of murder or manslaughter. Statutes from various states are provided as examples, but once again I admonish you to know what the laws are where you are carrying a concealed handgun. Two recent US Supreme Court decisions relating to the Second Amendment are summarized.

Suggested reading:

Branca, Andrew F. 2013. *The Law of Self-Defense: The Indispensable Guide for the Armed Citizen*. Maynard, Massachusetts: Law of Self-Defense.

Vilos, Mitch, and Evan Vilos. 2010. *Self-Defense Laws of All 50 States*. USA: Guns West.

Second Amendment

"A well-regulated Militia being necessary to the security of a free State, the right of the people to keep and bear Arms shall not be infringed."

The Second Amendment to the US Constitution, ratified with the Bill of Rights in 1791, guarantees the "individual" right to keep and bear arms. The right of the people to keep and bear arms is a restatement of the right to self-defense. The Second Amendment recognizes the right to not only protect oneself from criminal conduct, but also from a tyrannical state or federal government. It was the US Supreme Court *Heller* decision in 2008 that affirmed that the Second Amendment is an "individual" right as opposed to a "collective" right granted to a militia. It was the US Supreme Court *McDonald* decision in 2010 that affirmed that the Second Amendment applies to the states, not just the federal government.

Heller Decision

The *Heller* decision is an historic landmark US Supreme Court case in the favor of Dick Anthony Heller, a DC police officer who lived in Washington, DC, and who had applied to register a handgun he wished to keep at home. The District of Columbia refused his request. He then filed suit on Second Amendment grounds, and the DC District Court dismissed his suit. But the DC Circuit Court reversed that decision, holding that the Second Amendment to the US Constitution protects an individual's right to possess firearms.

Furthermore, the court held that the city's total ban on handguns, as well as its trigger-lock requirement that firearms in the home be kept nonfunctional even when necessary for self-defense, violated that right. Specifically, the US Supreme Court held as follows:

The Second Amendment protects an individual right to possess a firearm unconnected with service in a militia, and to use that arm for traditionally lawful purposes, such as self-defense within the home. The handgun ban [in effect in Washington, DC, since 1976] and the trigger-lock requirement (as applied to self-defense) violate the Second Amendment (U.S. Supreme Court. 2008. *District of Columbia v. Heller*, 554 U.S. 570).

McDonald **Decision**

Otis McDonald and three other Chicago residents wanted to keep handguns in their homes for self-defense because they lived in a high-crime neighborhood that had been overtaken by gangs and drug dealers. Chicago had gun laws effectively banning handgun possession by almost all private citizens. After the US Supreme Court's *Heller* decision, McDonald and other petitioners sought a declaration that the ban and other city ordinances violated the Second and Fourteenth Amendments to the US Constitution. In this landmark case, the Supreme Court considered whether the Second Amendment in the Bill of Rights applies to the individual US states. The US Supreme Court ruled that the Fourteenth Amendment due-process clause makes the Second Amendment right to keep and bear arms fully applicable to the states and struck down the Chicago handgun ban as unconstitutional (U.S. Supreme Court. 2010. *McDonald v. City of Chicago*, 561 U.S. 742).

Castle Doctrine

In criminal law, the legal principle known as the castle doctrine is an exception to the retreat rule that allows the use of deadly force by a person who is protecting his or her home and its inhabitants from attack. It applies in the case of a trespasser who intends to commit a felony or inflict serious bodily harm. Also termed *dwelling defense* or *defense of habitation* (BLD). See *retreat rule*.

Example 1: *Castle Doctrine in Massachusetts.* Massachusetts is a state that applies the castle doctrine. The applicable Massachusetts general law is as follows:

> *MGL Chapter 278: Section 8A. Killing or injuring a person unlawfully in a dwelling; defense.* Section 8A. In the prosecution of a person who is an occupant of a dwelling charged with killing or injuring one who was unlawfully in said dwelling, it shall be a defense that the occupant was in his dwelling at the time of the offense and that he acted in the reasonable belief that the person unlawfully in said dwelling was about to inflict *great bodily injury or death* upon said occupant or upon another person lawfully in said dwelling, and that said occupant used reasonable means to defend himself or such other person lawfully in said dwelling. There shall be *no duty on said occupant to retreat* from such person unlawfully in said dwelling.
> (Italics added) See *no-retreat rule.*

Example 2: *Castle Doctrine in Florida.* The castle doctrine applies if an intruder or an invited guest attacks you in your own home. In Florida, the castle doctrine also applies when you are in your place of business. If you are in danger of death or great bodily harm, or you are trying to prevent a forcible felony, you do not have to retreat before using deadly force in self-defense.

Danger Zone (Twenty-One-Foot Rule)

In the context of a self-defense situation, the twenty-one-foot rule refers to the maximum distance between a person with a holstered concealed handgun and an aggressor armed with a knife, ax, club, butcher's cleaver, or other weapon from which a person may be considered to be in danger of serious bodily harm or death. From twenty-one feet, the aggressor is expected to have sufficient time (approximately one and a half seconds) to get to a person before a holstered handgun can be drawn for self-protection. This distance is based on what is known as the Tueller drill or twenty-one-foot rule published in *SWAT* magazine in 1983. If an armed attacker is within twenty-one feet of you, he is well within your "danger zone" (Tueller 1983).

Deadly Force

Deadly force is a legal term that refers to violent action known to create a substantial risk of causing death or serious bodily harm. Generally, a person may use deadly force in self-defense or in defense of another only if defending against another's deadly force or threat of serious bodily harm.

Example 1: *Deadly Force in Connecticut.*

> *General Statutes of Connecticut, Section 53a-19.*
> *Use of physical force in defense of person.*
> Except as provided in subsections (b) and (c) of this section, a person is justified in using reasonable physical force upon another person to defend himself or a third person from what he reasonably believes to be the use or imminent use of physical force, and he may use such degree of force which he reasonably believes to be necessary for such purpose; except that deadly physical force may not be used unless the actor

reasonably believes that such other person is (1) using or about to use deadly physical force, or (2) inflicting or about to inflict great bodily harm.

The Connecticut statute above points out that there is a difference between "reasonable physical force" and "deadly physical force." The statute implies that an individual must respond proportionately depending upon the circumstances.

Example 2: *Deadly Force in Florida.*

> *Florida Statute 776.012 Use of force in defense of person.* A person is justified in the use of deadly force and does not have a duty to retreat if he or she reasonably believes that such force is necessary to prevent imminent death or great bodily harm to himself or herself or another or to prevent the imminent commission of a forcible felony.[10]

> *Florida Statute 776.013 Home protection; use of deadly force; presumption of fear of death or great bodily harm.* [This statute goes into great detail about when and under what circumstances deadly force would be justified.] For example, a person who is not engaged in an unlawful activity and who is attacked in any other place where he or she has a right to be has *no duty to retreat* and has the *right to stand his or her ground* and meet force with force, including deadly force if he or

---

10. This Florida statute informs us that, in general, there are only two reasons that justify use of deadly force in self-defense of your person: (1) a person must reasonably believe the other person is using or about to use deadly force, and (2) the other person is inflicting or about to inflict great bodily harm. There is a third circumstance that justifies use of deadly force, that is, "to prevent the imminent commission of a forcible felony." (See "forcible felony.")

she reasonably believes it is necessary to do so to prevent death or great bodily harm to himself or herself or another to prevent the commission of a forcible felony.[11]

Florida Statute 776.031 Use of force in defense of others. A person is justified in the use of deadly force *only* if he or she reasonably believes that such force is necessary to prevent the imminent commission of a *forcible felony*. A person does not have a duty to retreat if the person is in a place where he or she has a right to be.

Example 3: *Force in Defense of Habitation in Utah*

In Utah, a person is justified in using force intended or likely to cause death or serious bodily injury (i.e., "deadly force") only if the person reasonably believes that force is necessary to prevent death or serious bodily injury to the person or a third person as a result of another person's imminent use of unlawful force, or to prevent the commission of a forcible felony. Under Utah Statute 76-2-402, a forcible felony includes aggravated assault, murder, manslaughter, kidnapping, rape, forcible sodomy, rape of a child, sexual abuse of a child, sexual assault, arson, robbery, and burglary (Utah Statutes 76-2-402 and 76-2-405).[12]

These examples of Connecticut, Florida, and Utah statutes were chosen to exemplify states that have very clearly defined statutes. These examples are also intended to show that

---

11. Florida Statute 773.013 is an example of a well-defined stand-your-ground and no-duty-to-retreat law that also explicitly describes under what circumstances deadly force is justified.

12. Utah Statute 76-2-402 clearly defines forcible felony. A concealed carry holder, therefore, knows under what circumstances deadly force may be justified.

each state has its own version about when and under what circumstances use of deadly force is justified. The Florida and Utah statutes are very similar and have virtually the same criteria for use of deadly force. Many states do not have such detailed statutes, and as a result, a person who uses deadly force may be more vulnerable to prosecution.

The author highly recommends that any concealed-carry holder read all the applicable statutes of their resident state first. It is also suggested that if one intends to carry concealed handguns in another state, it is essential to know the applicable laws in that state as well. A very good starting point for a better understanding of the state-to-state legal similarities and differences is the book *Self-Defense Laws of All 50 States* by Mitch and Evan Vilos. Andrew Branca's book *The Law of Self-Defense* is also an excellent source. Branca also offers seminars on the self-defense laws of many of the states.

No-Retreat Rule

In criminal law, the no-retreat rule is the legal doctrine that the victim of a murderous assault may use deadly force in self-defense if there is no reasonable alternative to avoid the assailant's threatened harm (BLD).

Example: *No-Retreat Rule in Florida.* In Florida, a person who is not engaged in an unlawful activity and who is attacked in any other place where he or she has a right to be *has no duty to retreat* and has the *right to stand his or her ground* and meet force with force, including deadly force if he or she reasonably believes it is necessary to do so to prevent death or great bodily harm to himself or herself or another or to prevent the commission of a forcible felony. [This section of law applies to a dwelling, residence or an occupied vehicle.] (Florida Statute 776.013(d)(3)).

Retreat Rule

In criminal law, the retreat rule is the legal doctrine holding that the victim of an assault has a duty to retreat instead of resorting to deadly force in self-defense unless (1) the victim is at home or in his or her place of business (the so-called castle doctrine), or (2) the assailant is a person whom the victim is trying to arrest (BLD). See n*o-retreat rule*.

Stand-Your-Ground Law

A stand-your-ground law is a type of self-defense law that states that a person may justifiably use force in self-defense and has no duty to retreat first when there is reasonable belief of an unlawful threat. Whereas the castle doctrine generally applies to situations in the home or places of residence, stand your ground applies to any other place where one has a right to be and where one is not doing anything illegal. This type of law is common in multiple jurisdictions within the United States and exists in statutory law and in common law precedents. No duty to retreat is synonymous with the right to stand your ground.
See *no-retreat rule* and *castle doctrine*.

Historically, it was the 1895 Supreme Court case *Beard v. United States* that established a precedent for "standing your ground" for personal self-defense. Beard, a farmer, used a shotgun to defend himself against three armed men on his property who were trying to steal one of his cows. To protect himself from the aggressors and without firing a single shot, he struck one man in the head who appeared to be drawing a pistol. The blow to the head from the butt of the shotgun resulted in the man's death.

The Supreme Court ruled that *Beard* was assailed on his own grounds, without provocation, by a person armed with a deadly weapon and apparently seeking to kill him, and was not obliged to retreat. He was entitled to "stand his ground" and defend himself with such means as was within his control, so long as he intended no purpose of doing anything beyond what was necessary to save his own life. He was found not guilty of murder or manslaughter. (U.S. Supreme Court. 1895. *Beard v. United States*, 158 U.S. 550).

Example: *Stand-Your-Ground Law in Florida.* Florida's Statute 776.013 (revision 4/12) is an example of a stand-your-ground or no-retreat law.

Section 3 of that statute reads as follows:

> A person who is not engaged in an unlawful activity and who is attacked in any other place where he or she has a right to be has *no duty to retreat* and has the *right to stand his or her ground* and meet force with force, including deadly force if he or she reasonably believes it is necessary to do so to prevent death or great bodily harm to himself or herself or another or to prevent the commission of a forcible felony.

Section 4 of that statute reads as follows:

> A person who unlawfully and by force enters or attempts to enter a person's dwelling, residence, or occupied vehicle is presumed to be doing so with the intent to commit an unlawful act involving force or violence.[13]

---

13. Section 4 extends the zone of coverage beyond the home and specifically includes an occupied vehicle. Thus, stand your ground would apply in a carjacking situation in Florida.

Home Protection Strategy

A home protection plan prepares you to protect yourself and other family members from an aggressor who has broken into your home or is otherwise intending you harm within the confines of your home. There are many books, videos, and gun training courses that teach people ways to protect their family and loved ones should an aggressor enter their home. If one chooses to have a firearm in the house for self-defense, it is advisable to take a course or read a book on home defense strategy.

The *NRA Guide to the Basics of Personal Protection in the Home* is a good example, specifically chapter 14, "Responding to a Possible Break-In," and chapter 15, "Confronting an Intruder or Attacker." Depending upon the circumstances, basic home defense fundamentals include withdrawing to a safe room, such as the master bedroom, where you should have a telephone to call 911, a flashlight, and your firearm.

Here are some considerations for home defense that I have gleaned from my research. A handgun for home defense does not have to be concealed, so considerations such as size, weight, and barrel length are not critical issues as they are for concealed carry. Most handgun ammunition can penetrate materials used in home construction and will be able to punch through most walls and doors easily. It is advisable to engage an assailant in your home from a low position of cover so that any missed shots will go high and not penetrate adjoining rooms.

It is noteworthy that long guns, such as shotguns, are usually not the weapons of choice for home defense. The author recognizes there are exceptions to any general rule, but long guns, such as shotguns and rifles, are usually not recommended by experts and have many disadvantages. It is easier for an assailant to grab a long barrel in close encounters and disarm you.

Note about warning shots: Two shotgun blasts off your front porch is not considered an effective home protection strategy by experts. You could be committing a felony by doing so, and if your assailant(s) is not scared away, you are left standing there with an empty shotgun or one with two less rounds.

Suggested reading:

NRA. 2000. *NRA Guide to the Basics of Personal Protection in the Home.* Fairfax, Virginia: National Rifle Association.

Eckstine, Roger. 2014. *Shooter's Bible Guide to Home Defense.* Birmingham, AL: Palladium Press.

Carjacking

For concealed-carry holders, it is important to know that cars are considered property, and defense of property laws vary widely from state to state. Most states only allow use of reasonable force (not deadly force) to prevent the robbery of an occupied motor vehicle; that is, unless the driver is in fear of his life or great bodily harm—for example, if the assailant uses a gun. Readers should check their resident state laws to see if carjacking is explicitly covered in their state statutes, or if there is any precedent case law relating to carjacking.

Absent any specific statutory language on carjacking, the fallback justification for use of deadly force in self-defense while in a motor vehicle is presumed to be fear of death or great bodily harm that already exists in most state statutes. Louisiana is one state that has explicitly addressed carjacking in their statutes because of a high incidence of this crime in

New Orleans in the 1990s. For example, excerpts from the Louisiana statute for justifiable homicide read as follows:

A homicide is justifiable:

> (1) When committed in self-defense by one who reasonably believes that he is in imminent danger of losing his life or receiving great bodily harm and that the killing is necessary to save himself from that danger.
> (2) When committed for the purpose of preventing a violent or forcible felony involving danger to life or of great bodily harm by one who reasonably believes that such an offense is about to be committed and that such action is necessary for its prevention. The circumstances must be sufficient to excite the fear of a reasonable person that there would be serious danger to his own life or person if he attempted to prevent the felony without the killing.
> (2011 LA Rev Stat § 14:20)[14]

In December 2013 a man was killed at a New Jersey shopping mall during a carjacking. If he had been carrying a concealed handgun for personal protection, would he have been able to save himself? Nobody knows, but at least he might have had a chance.

---

14. For a detailed analysis of Louisiana's so-called "kill the carjacker" statute, see: Susan Michelle Gerling. "Louisiana's New 'Kill the Carjacker' Statute: Self-Defense or Instant Injustice?" 55 Washington University, *Journal of Urban and Contemporary Law* 109 (1999). http://openscholarship.wustl.edu/law_urbanlaw/vol55/iss1/6

Notorious Self-Defense Cases

Two widely publicized self-defense cases are mentioned here as illustrations of what can happen to a defendant after a shooting. Bernhard Goetz was charged with attempted murder and several firearm offenses and was sued in civil court for damages. George Zimmerman was tried for second degree murder.

Bernhard Goetz

On December 22, 1984, Bernhard Goetz shot four men who tried to mug him on a New York City subway train with his five-shot, .38-caliber revolver. He was charged with attempted murder, assault, reckless endangerment, and several firearms offenses. He was found not guilty of all charges except one of the firearms charges, for which he served less than a year in jail. One of the men who was shot became a paraplegic and won a civil suit against Goetz for $43 million.

There are three important observations concerning the facts in this self-defense case: (1) all four men survived being shot by a .38-caliber bullet(s), (2) using force in self-defense may result in your being charged with murder or attempted murder, and (3) maiming or killing someone in self-defense may result in your being sued in civil court for huge amounts of money for damages.

Suggested reading:

Fletcher, George P. *A Crime of Self Defense: Bernard Goetz and the Law on Trial*. Chicago: University of Chicago Press. 1988.

George Zimmerman

The George Zimmerman trial in Sanford, Florida, in July 2013 is a well-known self-defense case. Zimmerman, who was a neighborhood crime watchman, was charged by the State of Florida with second-degree murder of Trayvon Martin. Zimmerman said that he acted in self-defense "to prevent imminent death or great bodily harm." He suffered a broken nose and a bloody head injury from his head being slammed on a concrete sidewalk before he shot Trayvon Martin dead with one shot from a 9 mm Kel-Tec handgun. On July 13, 2013, Zimmerman was found not guilty because the prosecution failed to prove that he was guilty of second-degree murder or manslaughter beyond a reasonable doubt.

Massachusetts Gun Storage Law

The Commonwealth of Massachusetts has a firearm storage law that residents should be aware of for purposes of compliance, but also because it relates to the accessibility of a firearm for self-defense. MGL Chapter 140, Section 131L(a) reads verbatim as follows:

> Section 131L(a). It shall be unlawful to store or keep any firearm, rifle or shotgun including, but not limited to, large capacity weapons, or machine gun in any place unless such weapon is secured in a locked container or equipped with a tamper-resistant mechanical lock or other safety device, properly engaged so as to render such weapon inoperable by any person other than the owner or other lawfully authorized user. For purposes of this section, such weapon shall not be deemed stored or kept if carried by or under the control of the owner or other lawfully authorized user.

After the *Heller* Supreme Court case that involved a trigger lock requirement was adjudicated, there were two legal challenges to the constitutionality of the Massachusetts gun storage law 131L(a). These cases are summarized below. In both cases the constitutionality of 131L(a) was upheld.

Two Cases Involving Unsecured Guns at Home

Case 1: Massachusetts General Law Chapter 40, Section 131L(a)—Unsecured Guns in Home

In 2010 there was an interesting case in Greenfield, Massachusetts, relating to secure gun storage. Police searched a man's apartment and found four unsecured weapons including a .38-caliber revolver, a 9 mm pistol, a derringer, and a 12-gauge shotgun. The man filed suit, claiming that the Massachusetts law requiring residents to lock up their guns, even while they are in one's house, was unconstitutional in light of the *Heller* decision.

The Massachusetts court held that the law was still constitutional because:

> MGL c. 140, section 131L(a), does not require that firearms in the home be rendered and kept inoperable at all times and does not prohibit a licensed gun owner from carrying a loaded firearm in the home.

and,

> ...a gun owner may therefore carry or keep a loaded firearm in his or her home without securing it with a trigger lock or comparable safety device. The gun owner's obligation to secure the firearm in accordance with the statute arises only when the firearm is stored or

otherwise outside the owner's immediate control. (*Greenfield Recorder* December 4, 2010)

Case 2: Massachusetts Unsecured Gun in Nightstand at Home (Reference: SJC-11076, January 29, 2013 and 464 Mass.232)

The *Commonwealth of Massachusetts v. John McGowan* is a more recent case involving unsecure gun storage in the home. The defendant owned a Smith & Wesson .40-caliber semiautomatic handgun, which he kept loaded and unlocked in a bedroom side table drawer on the second floor of his home. The defendant had a valid license to carry a firearm in Massachusetts. That license was issued by the Springfield Police Department. Officers were dispatched to the defendant's house in response to a telephone call about a domestic disturbance.

When the police arrived, the defendant reported that he had had an argument with his female "roommate" over a ten-dollar loan, and that his roommate became angry, went into the defendant's bedroom, retrieved his loaded handgun from the unlocked drawer, left the house, threw the firearm into the bushes beside the neighboring house, and locked the defendant out of the house when he left to retrieve the weapon. The officers secured the handgun, which was loaded with ten rounds, one in the chamber and the remainder in the magazine. The defendant told police that the firearm was loaded that way when the roommate took it.

The defendant was charged in a criminal complaint with a violation of Massachusetts General Laws (MGL) Section 131L(a). The court again upheld the constitutionality of MGL Chapter 140, Section 131L(a). Specifically, the Supreme Judicial Court of Massachusetts concluded that:

> §131L(a) allows the owner of a firearm to carry or otherwise keep the firearm under the owner's

immediate control within the home, and where
the storage requirements are reasonably designed
to prevent persons who are not licensed to
possess or carry a firearm, including felons, the
mentally ill, and children, from getting illegal
access to a firearm, §131L(a) falls outside the
scope of the right to bear arms protected by the
Second Amendment.

Gun owners may carry or keep a loaded firearm under
their control in their home without securing it with a trigger
lock or comparable safety device. However, a gun owner's
obligation to secure a firearm in accordance with the law arises
when the firearm is stored, or is otherwise outside the owner's
immediate control.

Thus, unlike the provision declared unconstitutional in
Heller, Section 131L(a) was deemed consistent with the right
of self-defense in the home, because it does not interfere with
the ability of a licensed gun owner to carry or keep a loaded
firearm under his or her immediate control for self-defense.

In summary, the court determined that because Section
131L(a) is consistent with the right to bear arms in self-
defense in one's home and is designed to prevent those who
are not licensed to possess or carry firearms from gaining
access to firearms, Section 131L(a) is constitutional under the
US Supreme Court's holdings and analysis in *Heller* and
McDonald, and Massachusetts may enforce Section 131L(a) to
protect the health, safety, and welfare of its citizens.

These two cases relate to the very practical matter of
how does one store or keep a handgun in a house in
Massachusetts and also have it readily accessible for self-
defense at a moment's notice. One key issue is what
constitutes the owner's immediate or direct control. If one is at
home and leaves a handgun in a bedside drawer and then

leaves the room, is the handgun still under one's immediate or direct control? It depends. Could not somebody else, perhaps a child, go there and retrieve it? A gun is not under direct control if it is not on a person's body or in near proximity to enable that person to stop unauthorized access.

As a resident of Massachusetts, I pay particular attention to Section 131L(a). To keep a handgun under one's immediate or direct control and readily accessible, one has to keep it holstered on his or her person at all times. That means walking around the house with a holstered weapon at all times. That is not very practical or desirable. But leaving the handgun loaded in another room in a drawer is not under one's direct control.

How one stores or keeps a handgun in the house affects its accessibility for self-defense. Other than carrying a handgun around the house at all times, how does one comply with the Massachusetts state law and still have a firearm readily accessible at a moment's notice to respond to a life-threatening situation? One way is to keep a self-defense handgun locked up in a mini-safe that can be accessed in seconds. A biometric thumbprint lock or keylock may still require about five seconds to open if you are near it. A combination lock takes too much time so the handgun is not readily accessible.

The next chapter addresses federal firearms laws that relate to concealed-carry and self-defense.

Chapter 8

Federal Firearms Laws

*Each time the government creates new laws that regulate and
limit our access to firearms, we are one step closer to being a
disarmed and defenseless people, the very state of affairs the
Founding Fathers feared and sought to prevent.*
Judge Andrew P. Napolitano (2010)

Starting with the Second Amendment to the US
Constitution, chapter 8 summarizes some of the key federal
firearms laws that exist today, as well as the federal assault
weapons ban that expired in 2004. Federal gun control laws
and the federal law that regulates the interstate transportation
of firearms are described.

At this writing, it has been 225 years since the Second
Amendment was made a part of the US Constitution. Today
there are hundreds of federal gun laws regulating the
manufacture, sale, and possession of firearms. Owners of
firearms must comply with increasingly complex and
ambiguous laws, many that infringe on one's individual right
of self-defense.

In his book *Gun Laws of America* (1999), Alan Korwin
documented the growth in federal gun laws from 1791 to 1998.
The Second Amendment itself contains only twenty-seven
words. During those years a total of 88,584 words in federal
gun laws have been added by the federal government. For
comparison purposes, this book contains approximately 45,000
words.

Second Amendment

The Second Amendment to the US Constitution, ratified with the Bill of Rights in 1791, was intended to ensure that a citizen's right to keep and bear arms would not be infringed by the federal government. The Founding Fathers, including Thomas Jefferson, Samuel Adams, John Madison, Noah Webster, George Mason, and Patrick Henry, recognized the right of American citizens to possess their own firearms. Madison proclaimed that the fact that Americans were armed was an advantage over the people of almost every other nation.

The right to keep and bear arms is a restatement of the ancient natural right to self-defense; it recognizes not only the right to protect oneself from criminal conduct, but also from a tyrannical state or federal government (Napolitano 2010).

As Judge Napolitano asserts in his book, the federal government did not infringe upon this fundamental liberty until the early twentieth century, justifying that guns cause violence and death and that gun control results in lower crime and safer streets.

As discussed in chapter 7, two very important US Supreme Court decisions concerning the Second Amendment and the right to bear arms for self-defense were passed within the last ten years. The US Supreme Court's *Heller* decision in 2008 affirmed that the Second Amendment is an "individual" right as opposed to a "collective" right granted to a militia. The US Supreme Court's *McDonald* decision in 2010 affirmed that the Second Amendment applies to the states, not just the federal government.

Suggested reading:

Adams, Les. 1996. *The Second Amendment Primer: A Citizen's Guidebook to the History, Sources, and Authorities for the Constitutional Guarantee of the Right to Keep and Bear Arms.* Birmingham, Alabama: Palladium Press.

Napolitano, Andrew P. 2010. *Lies the Government Told You* (p. 94-119). Nashville, Tennessee: Thomas Nelson.

Sommers, Michael A. 2001. *Individual Rights and Civic Responsibility: The Right to Bear Arms.* New York: The Rosen Publishing Group.

Gun-Control Law (General Definition)

A gun-control law is any statute or ordinance that regulates the sale, possession, or use of firearms. Gun-control laws vary widely among the states, and many cities have gun-control ordinances. Federal law restricts and regulates the illegal sale, possession, and use of firearms (18 U.S.C.A. § 921–930).

The *United States Code* (U.S.C.)

The *United States Code* is the official name for US federal laws. Federal laws, which are also known as federal statutes, are organized into a set of fifty numbered "titles" that make up the *United States Code*. The most important federal gun laws are contained under title 18, "Crimes and Criminal Procedures." Federal laws within the U.S.C. are designated by a numbering system that identifies the title, section, subsection, paragraph, and subparagraph. For example, the citation 18 U.S.C. § 922 (v & w) means title 18 of the *United States Code*, section 922, subsections v and w.

The *United States Code Annotated* (U.S.C.A.)

The *United States Code Annotated* is a multivolume publication of the complete text of the *United States Code* with historical notes, cross-references, and case notes of federal and state decisions construing specific code sections (BLD).

National Firearms Act of 1934

The National Firearms Act of 1934 is a major federal gun law that was adopted in response to the gangster activity of the Prohibition era. The law imposed tax and registration requirements on "gangster weapons." The law is found in title 26 of the Internal Revenue Service laws. This act primarily regulates machine guns, rifles, and shotguns, but also includes "a pistol or revolver having a barrel with a smooth bore designed or redesigned to fire a fixed shotgun shell" (26 U.S.C. § 5845).

Gun Control Act of 1968

The Gun Control Act of 1968 is a federal gun law that was enacted in the aftermath of various political assassinations in the 1960s, including those of John F. Kennedy, Robert F. Kennedy, and Martin Luther King. It prohibited all sales of guns through the mail, placed restrictions on sales between states, and prohibited certain individuals, such as felons and the mentally impaired, from owning firearms (18 U.S.C. § 922).

Interstate Transportation of Firearms

The federal law regulating the interstate transportation of firearms is known as the McClure-Volkmer Act of 1986. This federal law, also known as the "safe passage" provision of the Firearm Owners Protection Act, is intended to protect persons traveling from one state to another from being arrested and incarcerated for a firearms offense in a state that has strict gun control laws. The law reads as follows:

> Notwithstanding any other provision of any law or any rule or regulation of a State or any political subdivision thereof, any person who is not otherwise prohibited by this chapter from transporting, shipping, or receiving a firearm shall be entitled to transport a firearm for any lawful purpose from any place where he may lawfully possess and carry such firearm to any other place where he may lawfully possess and carry such firearm if, during such transportation the firearm is unloaded, and neither the firearm nor any ammunition being transported is readily accessible or is directly accessible from the passenger compartment of such transporting vehicle: Provided, That in the case of a vehicle without a compartment separate from the driver's compartment the firearm or ammunition shall be contained in a locked container other than the glove compartment or console (18 U.S.C. § 926A).

I will assess this federal law from two perspectives: (1) its effectiveness for its intended purpose (i.e., to protect persons traveling from state to state from unlawful arrest and prosecution); and (2) its infringement upon the right of individuals to carry a loaded firearm for self-defense. As I will show by the following example, this federal law does not always work the way it was intended.

Take the case of *Gregg C. Revell vs. Port Authority of New York and New Jersey*. In March 2005 Revell, a resident of Utah, was traveling by air from Salt Lake City (SLC) to Allentown, Pennsylvania, a trip that included a stop in Newark, New Jersey. At the SLC airport, Revell checked a firearm and ammunition in separate, hard, locked cases in accordance with federal regulations.

Revell's flight to Newark was late, and he missed his connecting flight from Newark to Allentown. He then tried booking another flight that evening, but the airline decided to make arrangements to bus passengers to Allentown instead. Due to a baggage problem, Revell missed the bus and ended up staying overnight at a Newark airport hotel. The next morning he went to the Newark airport to book another flight to Allentown. There he proceeded to the ticket counter to check his baggage and declare his firearm and ammunition.

Revell indicated that he was merely passing through New Jersey; however, he was held for violation of New Jersey firearm statutes, handcuffed, arrested, held in jail overnight, transferred to another jail, and incarcerated another three days until he was released on bond. Four months later the charges against him were dismissed. He did not get his gun and ammunition back until more than two years after the ill-fated trip. If the federal law had worked as intended, he should never have been arrested and charged (Glidden and Collins 2013).

In addition to being ineffective for its intended purpose (i.e., avoidance of legal jeopardy), this law actually infringes on a person's right to bear firearms for self-defense. The "safe passage" law requires that any transported firearm must be *unloaded*, and that any firearm or any ammunition must *not be readily accessible*. As firearm experts know, for purposes of concealed carry and self-defense, a firearm must be loaded and immediately accessible. If someone intending harm walks up to a vehicle and starts shooting at the occupant(s), under this law any firearm in the vehicle is not readily available for self-defense. In many conceivable situations, only seconds are available to access and use a firearm for self-defense. See *twenty-one-foot rule*.

Although this law does allow for the transportation of legally possessed, unloaded firearms, it does not enable the accessible use of any of those firearms in a self-defense situation. It must be assumed then that the controlling law that would allow concealed carry would be the state law of the state you were in. If you had a concealed-carry permit for that state, then you would be authorized to have a loaded firearm on your person or readily accessible. Thus, if you are traveling through ten different states, you either have to have a concealed-carry license for each state that you drive through, or your resident concealed-carry permit must be recognized by those states.

What happened in this case in New Jersey may have occurred because law enforcement officials were either unaware of the McClure-Volkmer Act or did not understand its purpose. The federal law itself was not only ineffective for its intended purpose, but it precludes anyone from carrying a loaded firearm in their vehicle for self-defense.

Both of these situations can only be remedied by a federal law that provides for a universal reciprocity of valid concealed-carry permits. It must be a law given national attention and all the states should strictly adhere to it. Remember that driving a car is a privilege, while the right to bear arms for self-defense is a constitutional right. People are legally permitted to drive from state to state on one driver's license. The same should apply for a concealed-carry permit.

Brady Act

The Brady Act is a federal law establishing a national system for quickly checking the background of a prospective handgun purchaser. The formal name of the law is the Brady Handgun Violence Prevention Act of 1994 (18 U.S.C.A. § 921–930). The Brady Act was signed into law by President Bill Clinton in 1994 and instituted federal background checks and waiting periods on firearms purchasers in the United States. The act was named after James Brady, who was shot by John Hinckley Jr. during an attempted assassination of President Ronald Reagan in 1981.

The effectiveness of background checks and waiting periods for handgun purchases is still a controversial gun control issue today. In the book *Freakonomics*, authors Levitt and Dubner point out that the Brady Act may have appealed to politicians, but it makes little sense to an economist. Why? Because there is a huge black market for handguns that are so cheap and easy to get that a criminal has no incentive to fill out a firearms application at a gun store. In fact, one study of imprisoned felons has shown that only one-fifth of criminals bought their guns through a licensed gun dealer.

Large-Capacity Ammunition-Feeding Device

A large-capacity device is a magazine, belt, drum, feed strip, or similar device manufactured after the date of enactment of the Violent Crime Control and Law Enforcement Act of 1994 that has a capacity of, or that can be readily restored or converted to accept, more than ten rounds of ammunition (18 U.S.C. § 921).

National Instant Criminal Background Check System (NICS)

The NICS is a system for determining eligibility of an individual to purchase a firearm. Federally registered firearms dealers are required by law to use the NICS to determine if it is legal to sell a firearm to a prospective buyer. See *Brady Act*.

In his book *Crippled America*, presidential candidate Donald Trump points out that the national background check system is a complete failure. In his view, few criminals are stupid enough to try to pass a background check or have their names in any kind of system. They obtain their guns "by stealing them or buying them from an unlicensed source or getting them from family and friends." (Trump 2015).

School Zone Prohibition

According to federal law, it is unlawful for any individual to possess a firearm in a school zone (18 U.S.C. § 922(q)(2)). *School zone* means "(a) in, or on the grounds of, a public, parochial or private school; or (b) within a distance of 1,000 feet from the grounds of a public, parochial or private school (18 U.S.C. § 921 (a)(25))." However, there is an exception if the individual possessing the firearm is licensed to carry by the state (18 U.S.C. § 922(q)(2)(B)(ii)).

Federal Assault Weapons Ban (Expired)

The Violent Crime Control and Law Enforcement Act of 1994, Public Law 103-322, was a federal law in the United States that included a prohibition on the manufacture of certain semiautomatic firearms, so-called "assault weapons." The ten-year ban was passed by the US Congress and signed into law by President Bill Clinton. The ban applied only to weapons manufactured after the date of the ban's enactment, and it expired on September 13, 2004, as part of the law's sunset provision (18 U.S.C. § 922 (v & w)).

Certain types of semiautomatic pistols may fall under the definition of an assault weapon. A semiautomatic assault weapon as it pertains to handguns was defined in the federal Public Safety and Recreational Firearms Use Protection Act, 18 U.S.C. § 921(a)(30) as appearing in such section on September 13, 1994:

> (30) The term "semiautomatic assault weapon" means
> (C) a semiautomatic pistol that has an ability to accept a detachable magazine and has at least 2 of—
> (i) an ammunition magazine that attaches to the pistol outside of the pistol grip;
> (ii) a threaded barrel capable of accepting a barrel extender, flash suppressor, forward handgrip, or silencer;
> (iii) a shroud that is attached to, or partially or completely encircles, the barrel and that permits the shooter to hold the firearm with the nontrigger hand without being burned;
> (iv) a manufactured weight of 50 ounces or more when the pistol is unloaded; and
> (v) a semiautomatic version of an automatic firearm.

The federal ban on assault weapons in the United States expired in 2004.

However, the Commonwealth of Massachusetts incorporated the language of the federal assault weapons ban into their statutes and made it their state law. The Massachusetts "assault weapons" ban reads as follows:

> Chapter 140: Section 131M. Assault weapon or large capacity feeding device not lawfully possessed on September 13, 1994; sale, transfer or possession; punishment
> Section 131M. No person shall sell, offer for sale, transfer or possess an assault weapon or a large capacity feeding device that was not otherwise lawfully possessed on September 13, 1994. Whoever not being licensed under the provisions of section 122 violates the provisions of this section shall be punished, for a first offense, by a fine of not less than $1,000 nor more than $10,000 or by imprisonment for not less than one year nor more than ten years, or by both such fine and imprisonment, and for a second offense, by a fine of not less than $5,000 nor more than $15,000 or by imprisonment for not less than five years nor more than 15 years, or by both such fine and imprisonment.

On April 17, 2013, US Senator Diane Feinstein (D-CA) attempted to pass another federal version of an assault weapons ban in the aftermath of the Newtown massacre. The Feinstein bill would have banned the future manufacturing, possession, and sale of 157 semiautomatic weapons and high-capacity magazines. The bill was defeated in the US Senate by a vote of sixty to forty (*C-SPAN Live* 2013).

Undetectable Firearms Act of 1988

The Undetectable Firearms Act of 1988 is intended to improve the effectiveness of airport security metal detectors and airport security x-ray systems in detecting firearms that could be smuggled aboard aircraft by terrorists. The act amended section 922 of title 18 of the *United States Code* by adding at the end the following:

> (p)(l) It shall be unlawful for any person to manufacture, import, sell, ship, deliver, possess, transfer, or receive any firearm—
>
> (A) that, after removal of grips, stocks, and magazines, is not as detectable as the Security Exemplar, by walk-through metal detectors calibrated and operated to detect the Security Exemplar; or
>
> (B) any major component of which, when subjected to inspection by the types of x-ray machines commonly used at airports, does not generate an image that accurately depicts the shape of the component. Barium sulfate or other compounds may be used in the fabrication of the component.

This act was extended for ten more years effective December 9, 2013.

Confiscation

In general, confiscation is defined as the seizure of property by an authority. Confiscation of legally possessed firearms by a state or federal government is prohibited by the Second Amendment to the US Constitution. Although at least two US senators and one Supreme Court justice have advocated the universal confiscation of pistols, so far no federal law has passed in the United States Congress to confiscate all pistols. However, there is some precedent, and lessons can be learned from what occurred in Germany in the 1930s. See Holbrook 2000.

Example 1: *Gun Confiscation in Germany by the Nazis (1933).* The *New York Times* reported the following:

> Breslau, Apr 21. The Police President of the city has decreed that "all persons now or formerly of the Jewish faith who hold permits to carry arms or shooting licenses must surrender them forthwith to the police authorities." ("Permission to Possess Arms Withdrawn from Breslau Jews," April 23, 1933)

Example 2: *Quote from Supreme Court Justice Douglas.* In his dissenting opinion in *Adams v. Williams* (407 U.S. 143 (1972)), Justice William O. Douglas wrote, "There is no reason why all pistols should not be barred to everyone except the police."

I can think of many. Be wary. Confiscation is the first step to disarming a nation and leaving its people defenseless. Registration is viewed by many as a first step to confiscation. See *registration.*

Constitutional Concealed Carry Reciprocity Act

US Senator John Cornyn (R-Texas) introduced a bill (S. 498) in the US Senate of the 114th Congress on February 12, 2015, cited as the Constitutional Concealed Carry Reciprocity Act of 2015. This bill, if enacted, would allow reciprocity for the carrying of certain concealed firearms. This act would authorize an individual who has a valid license or permit in their resident state to carry a concealed firearm in any other state.

A companion bill, H.R. 923, was introduced in the US House of Representatives by Representative Marlin Stuzman (R-Indiana). This bipartisan measure would do away with the patchwork of state reciprocity laws and establish a uniform right to carry concealed firearms across all fifty states.

Similar measures in 2009, 2011, and 2013 have been tried and have not passed. However, support has been growing. Donald Trump, a 2016 presidential candidate as of this writing, has stated that he is "in favor of making all concealed-carry permits valid in every state" (Trump 2015). He said while campaigning that perhaps the body counts in active shootings, such as the one in Paris, could be reduced if more people are carrying concealed firearms.

The next chapter addresses some of the states' firearms laws that relate to concealed carry and self-defense and some recent trends in gun control legislation.

Chapter 9

State Firearms Laws and Gun Control

No anti-gun law ever disarmed a criminal; only respectable
people are rendered helpless.
Elmer Keith

Gun control is like trying to reduce drunk driving by making it
tougher for sober people to own cars.
Unknown

Chapter 9 addresses the controversial and bitterly contested issue of gun control. With the recent increase in deadly shootings in the United States, many states are passing more restrictive gun control measures while, on the other hand, some states are passing laws to make concealed carry more favorable. This chapter provides a general discussion of gun control and highlights some recent trends in state legislation.

By definition, a gun control law is any statute or ordinance that regulates the sale, possession, or use of firearms. The efforts of legislators to reduce crime by passing more gun control laws are many times not founded on any logical or scientific basis. Usually, gun laws are based on politics and many times are passed in reaction to a particularly gruesome mass shooting. More and more gun laws are being passed, and yet mass shootings are on the rise. Some government officials have even called for the confiscation of all handguns as if that would be a panacea to the gun violence.

Most of the current legislation measures can be grouped into two basic categories. First, there are those that are new, more restrictive gun control laws that have been passed by several states. On the other hand, several states have introduced new legislation that pushes back against more restrictive gun control laws. In essence, these two different categories (which happen to align with "political" factions) take opposite approaches in an attempt to prevent future mass shootings. In general, Democrats in state legislatures and the US Congress are more likely to favor more restrictive gun control, while Republicans are more likely to support gun laws that are less restrictive and more favorable to law-abiding gun owners and self-defense.

The recent state efforts on gun control that follow are representative examples of the two trends mentioned above. Gun control remains a highly political issue. The "more restrictive" legislators and their supporters believe that passing more restrictive gun control laws will result in fewer guns, and fewer guns will result in reduced gun violence. The "fewer restrictions" legislators and supporters believe that private citizens have a constitutional right to be armed for self-defense and that armed citizens may be able to save lives and stop active shootings in progress.

State "Assault Weapons" Bans

Although the federal "assault weapons" ban expired in 2004 and renewed attempts by Senator Feinstein in 2013 failed, some states and Washington, DC, still have such bans that are based on the original federal ban. In 2004 Massachusetts took language verbatim from the expired federal ban and made it their state law. Connecticut passed its own version of an assault weapons ban in April 2013 in the aftermath of the Newtown shooting at the Sandy Hook Elementary School. Connecticut adopted the same definition for "semiautomatic assault weapon" pistols as Massachusetts, taken verbatim from 18 U.S.C. 921(a)(30) above. Under Connecticut Statute section 53-202c, possession of an "assault weapon" is prohibited and is a felony. There are currently seven states and the District of Columbia that have assault weapons bans: California, Connecticut, Hawaii, Maryland, Massachusetts, New Jersey, and New York.

Pushback Against More Gun Control

Some states (Arkansas, Ohio, and Utah) have taken action in the aftermath of the Newtown and Aurora shootings to enable teachers to carry concealed firearms in schools to defend themselves and their students. Georgia has passed a law reducing the restrictions on no-carry places. There is also some pushback against anti-gun politicians in state legislatures.

Arkansas, Ohio, and Utah Teachers

At Clarksville High School in Arkansas, more than twenty teachers have taken firearms training and will be carrying concealed 9 mm handguns during school hours. This action is in response to the Newtown shooting in Connecticut (Johnston 2013). This action may be considered a realization that gun-free school zones are a myth in that only crazed mass murderers seem to have guns in school zones.

In forty Ohio school districts teachers with concealed carry licenses that undergo extended training will be allowed to carry concealed firearms in schools to defend themselves and their students in case an event like the Sandy Hook shooting occurs (Hawkins 2015).

Utah public teachers are also now allowed to carry concealed guns and parents are not allowed to find out who's carrying. (Hayden 2015).

Missouri Legislation

Missouri legislation was introduced that would declare invalid any federal policies that infringe on the Second Amendment. The law would allow state misdemeanor charges to be brought against federal agents who enforce such policies and anyone who publishes the identity of a gun owner. The bill would also lower Missouri's concealed handgun permit age to nineteen instead of twenty-one; and would allow specially trained teachers or administrators to serve as "school protection officers" to carry a concealed handgun (Lieb 2013).

Colorado Recall Elections

Two Colorado State senators were booted from office in recall elections due to their support for new gun control laws. The two Democratic senators favored new laws that subject private gun sales to background checks and ban magazines that hold more than fifteen rounds. The recall results are seen as pushback to tighter gun control laws and government overreach (Jones 2013).

Georgia's "Safe Carry Protection Act"

Georgia Governor Nathan Deal signed a law that makes it legal for licensed gun owners to carry concealed handguns in bars, schools, churches, and some government buildings that don't have security measures. This law may have been enacted as a response to an incident in Suwanee, Georgia, where a person took five firefighters hostage knowing they were unarmed (Copeland and Richards 2014).

California *(Peruta v. County of San Diego)*

In California in 2009 Edward Peruta was denied his application for a concealed carry license. Peruta subsequently sued the County of San Diego and its sheriff arguing that by denying him the ability to carry a loaded handgun for self-defense, the County infringed his right to bear arms under the Second Amendment. In 2014 the Ninth Circuit's decision affirmed the right of law-abiding citizens to carry handguns for lawful protection in public (Kopel 2014).

More Restrictive Gun Control

Some states (New York, Maryland, Colorado and Connecticut) have passed more restrictive firearms laws in the aftermath of the Newtown and Aurora shootings, some of which place limits on magazine capacity. Other more restrictive gun control measures being considered include new registration or licensing requirements, more background checks, confiscation of firearms, microstamping, or smart gun technology

Magazine Capacity

New York's Secure Ammunition and Firearms Enforcement (SAFE) Act of 2013[15] created a ban on any magazine that holds more than seven rounds. Subsequently, Federal District Court judge William Skretny ruled New York's magazine capacity limit of seven bullets violated the Second Amendment and was deemed unconstitutional (Loesch 2014).

Maryland's Firearm Safety Act of 2013 reduced the legal magazine capacity from twenty to ten rounds. In Colorado magazines that can hold more than fifteen rounds are prohibited by Colorado Revised Statute C.R.S. 18-12-302. In Connecticut magazines holding more than ten rounds of ammunition are banned. These magazine capacity limits were enacted despite lack of any evidence that such limits will do anything to stop mass shootings, or reduce body counts.

---

15. New gun control laws can also impact local economies and jobs. The Remington firearms manufacturer is expanding its manufacturing at a facility in Huntsville, Alabama, and that is expected to create three thousand new jobs. A union official for Remington in New York blames new gun control laws (the SAFE Act) for the move ("Remington Expands into Alabama after New York Enacts Strict Gun Laws," *The Daily Caller*, February 17, 2014).

To the contrary in 2014 New Jersey Governor Chris Christie vetoed legislation that would have banned possession of ammunition magazines with a capacity of more than ten rounds (the current limit is fifteen rounds.) Christie stated, "It simply defies common sense to believe that imposing a new and entirely arbitrary number of bullets that can be lawfully loaded into a firearm will somehow eradicate, or even reduce, future instances of mass violence."

On October 17, 1991 there was a mass killing in Killeen, Texas (Chin 1991) that demonstrated that magazine capacity limits have little if any effect on a murderous outcome. Madman George Hennard drove his pickup truck through a plate glass window into Luby's Café and started executing people at point blank range. He used two semi-automatic pistols to kill twenty-three people and wound twenty-seven others. During the shooting Hennard "paused methodically to reload his weapons and continue the slaughter" firing 61 rounds from one handgun and 41 rounds from the other until he finally committed suicide (Kasler 1992).

Universal Background Checks and Registration

Another disturbing trend in some of the states is the new laws for "universal background checks" (which means that private sales, even among family members, may have to go through a federal check), mandatory registration for every gun purchase, or other more restrictive licensing requirements that only make it more difficult for law-abiding citizens to purchase handguns for self-defense. There have even been discussions of confiscation of firearms in New York and New Jersey (Miller 2013).

Microstamping in California

In California a new gun law requires that "microstamping" technology be employed on handguns.

Firearm microstamping, also known as ballistic imprinting, engraves a microscopic marking on the tip of the firing pin that will leave an identifiable imprint on a bullet casing. Critics argue the microstamping technology is not perfected, is unreliable, serves no safety purpose, is cost prohibitive, and is not proven to aid in preventing or solving crimes (Chiaramonte 2014).

Suggested reading:

Michel, C.D. Chuck. 2013. *California Gun Laws: A Guide to State and Federal Firearm Regulations*. Long Beach, California: Coldaw.

"Smart" Guns

Some gun control advocates are promoting "smart gun" technology as a panacea to prevent the unlawful use of firearms. So-called "smart guns" are firearms that use electronics, batteries, and other technical means that require fingerprint identification and approval before a gun can be fired. This is intended to prevent children and criminals from being able to use the gun.

The problem with smart gun technology is that it is unreliable and has many functional issues. Conventional firearms are designed to withstand extreme environments, such as high and low temperatures, dirt, shock and impact, and moisture, even getting run over by motor vehicles. For example, Glock pistols have been put through a series of torture tests (PTOOMA 2004). These types of environments cause failure in electronic equipment, making a firearm much less reliable or useless in case of an emergency for self-defense.

So are smart guns really a smart idea? Today's mechanical-based firearms have near 100 percent reliability.

Why change that for something less reliable with no proven safety benefits? A better solution would be to store firearms in safes to prevent unauthorized access.

William B. Ruger Jr. on Gun Control

Here is some perspective from gun manufacturer William Ruger relating to gun control that appeared in the *New York Times* in 1994 (Wilson 2007, 282):

> The people who focus on gun control have got it all wrong. They are frustrated—we are all frustrated—but the quick fix they want just doesn't exist. They need to face reality. Criminals will always get guns...

> To find real answers to why there are deaths, we must look first at what is happening in American society, not the firearms business. Why have we lost our moral compass and become so lawless?...

> Of course we're concerned any time one of our guns shows up on a crime report. But passing more gun laws is not going to stop crime or criminals. As long as criminals are around, they'll have guns.

Readers should think over for themselves which approach is more likely to save lives in the event of a mass shooting. Given all the laws in existence already, it is my view that William Ruger was right. All the gun laws in the world will not stop bad people from getting them.

Vermont—the Ideal Second Amendment State?

In his book *Traveler's Guide to the Firearms Laws of the Fifty States (2013)*, J. Scott Kappas rates each state's gun laws on a scale from zero to 100 percent. A zero percent rating represents "total prohibition" meaning the state has extremely restrictive gun laws. A state with a 100 percent rating represents "total freedom" because the state has very minimal gun laws restricting the right to bear arms.

Vermont is a state with a 98 percent rating, the highest rating given. Only Alaska and Arizona have a rating as high as Vermont's. Vermont does not require individuals to have a license to carry concealed handguns. Individuals may carry loaded concealed handguns almost anywhere in the state with a few exceptions (courthouses, schools, and "state institutions"). The applicable Vermont statutes are as follows:

> *13 V.S.A. § 4003. Carrying dangerous weapons.* A person who carries a dangerous or deadly weapon, openly or concealed, with the intent or avowed purpose of injuring a fellow man, or who carries a dangerous or deadly weapon within any state institution or upon the grounds or lands owned or leased for the use of such institution, without the approval of the warden or superintendent of the institution, shall be imprisoned not more than two years or fined not more than $200.00, or both.[16]

> *13 V.S.A. § 4004. Possession of dangerous or deadly weapon in a school bus or school building*

---

16. What I find very interesting with this statute is that it is the "intent" or "avowed purpose" of an individual that determines criminality. The carrying of the gun by itself is not a crime. Basically, this statute uses the same reasoning as the maxim, "Guns don't kill people; people kill people."

or on school property. (a) No person shall knowingly possess a firearm or a dangerous or deadly weapon while within a school building or on a school bus.

13 V.S.A. § 4016. Weapons in court... (d) No dangerous or deadly weapon shall be allowed in a courthouse that has been certified by the court administrator to be a secured building.

In comparison, the highly gun-regulated state of Massachusetts was given a rating of 14 percent, the lowest rating of any state. What happened to Massachusetts? In 1775 Massachusetts was a cradle of liberty. The Battles of Lexington and Concord and "the shot heard round the world" have been symbols of freedom and liberty ever since. Today with respect to gun laws Massachusetts is the least free and most restrictive state in the US.

Throughout this book I have provided a brief look at the complexity and difficulty with some of today's guns laws, as well as how our Second Amendment right has been infringed. In Chapter 10 that follows I make a case for constitutional concealed carry and reciprocity in the US to enable qualified and certified US citizens to carry concealed firearms for self-defense purposes in all states.

Chapter 10

A Case for Universal Reciprocity

Well, a gun that's unloaded and cocked ain't good for nothin'.
Rooster Cogburn, *True Grit* (1969)

Neither is one that's unloaded and locked up in your car trunk.
Author

Chapter 10 addresses the need for constitutional concealed carry and reciprocity to enable qualified and certified US citizens to carry concealed firearms for self-defense in all 50 states. My personal experience is a primary reason why I wrote this book and why I advocate a national Constitutional Concealed Carry Reciprocity Act. Without such legislation, it is virtually impossible to exercise your right to carry concealed handguns for self-defense throughout the United States. With the high frequency of gun violence and active shootings in the US it is prudent to have armed citizens in places where they may act against the aggressors.

Second Amendment Infringement

The Second Amendment to the US Constitution states that "the right of the people to keep and bear arms shall not be infringed." To "infringe" as defined by *Webster* means "to violate or go beyond the limits of." An infringement is an encroachment of a privilege or right. To "encroach" is to intrude gradually on the rights or possessions of another. In recent years the federal and state governments have infringed and encroached upon the right of the people to bear arms for self-defense purposes.

As was noted earlier, two US Supreme Court decisions reaffirmed the Second Amendment right of an individual to "keep and bear arms." First the *Heller* decision (2008) legally resolved the ambiguity about whether the Second Amendment protects an "individual" or a "collective" right. *Heller* confirmed that the Second Amendment guarantees an individual's right to bear arms for self-defense purposes. Secondly, the *McDonald* decision (2010) held that the Second Amendment is applicable to the states as well as the federal government. These two decisions are important to keep in mind as I describe how the federal government and some specific states have infringed upon our Second Amendment right to self-defense and are continuing to do so today.

The Cost of Concealed Carry

For twenty years I was a resident of Reston, Virginia during the time I was working for the Pentagon. I bought my first handgun in Virginia in 2000 right after the Million Mom March in Washington, DC, that was calling for tighter gun control. I made the purchase as my own protest against the MOM rally. Shortly thereafter, I took a firearm safety and concealed-carry certification course at the NRA Headquarters. This enabled me to obtain a Virginia resident concealed-carry handgun permit.

During this time, I also owned a home in Massachusetts, a state that is renowned for its tough gun laws. My first difficulty occurred when I decided to get a license to carry in Massachusetts. Even though I owned a home in Massachusetts, my primary residence was Virginia (based on where I filed my income taxes). Therefore, I was not eligible to obtain a Massachusetts *resident* license, which costs only one hundred dollars and is valid for six years. Instead, I had to go through all the hoops for obtaining a *nonresident* license to carry in Massachusetts so that I could possess and carry guns in my second home.

In applying for the nonresident concealed-carry license in Massachusetts, I had to fill out forms and authorize release of local and state police records, have fingerprints taken, and provide a recent photo. I also had to submit a lengthy application form. The nonresident license cost me one hundred dollars for *one* year, plus all associated costs that amounted to about another fifty dollars per year. I had to travel twenty miles to Fairfax and take time off from work (more cost) to fill out more forms and get fingerprinted. The entire application process took between one and two weeks depending upon mailing and processing times. I also had to renew my Massachusetts nonresident license *every year* and provide the same documentation each year.

All this paperwork and time off from work had to be done just to exercise my constitutional right to possess handguns in my house in Massachusetts. Over nine years my total cost for a nonresident Massachusetts LTC was approximately $10,000. Another (not minor) problem was that the license itself was the size of an enlarged dollar bill that would not fit properly in a normal-sized wallet without sticking out more than half an inch.

State-to-State Issues

The various gun laws of all fifty of the United States do not currently allow for the authorized, uniform concealed carry of a handgun across state lines, even if a person has a valid concealed license to carry (LTC) in their resident state. The existing state of affairs of reciprocity and recognition of LTC or CCW permits among the states is very complicated and tedious to understand. There are contradictory, ambiguous, and confounding gun laws that are dubious in their purpose.

Some states do not issue nonresident concealed-carry permits (e.g., New York). Therefore, getting a concealed-carry license in such a state is not an option. One cannot carry a concealed firearm in one of these states for self-defense purposes if visiting that state.

If one were planning to drive across the United States by car, it is virtually impossible to legally carry a concealed handgun for self-defense. Inevitably, you would cross into a state where your resident license would not be valid.

The McClure-Volkmer Act (or safe passage law) that regulates the interstate transportation of firearms does not authorize concealed carry. This law explicitly states that the firearms being transported from state to state must be unloaded and locked up and not readily accessible. This condition makes the firearm unavailable for immediate self-defense.

There is also some question whether all states will even recognize this federal law. Remember the Revell case in New Jersey. Were the state authorities even aware of the safe passage federal law or did they just ignore it? This law is intended to protect you from overly restrictive state gun laws, but it is not guaranteed to do so. If one is traveling with a firearm from state to state, it might be prudent to have a copy of the law handy.

Contradictory Concealed-Carry Restrictions

Still another issue one may encounter relates to restrictions on concealed carry (i.e., places where you cannot carry) that vary from state to state. Since there is variation in the laws from state to state, some of these laws may be in contradiction, placing a burden on the carry holder to know the differences.

One example I encountered while living in Virginia was that you could not carry a concealed handgun into an establishment where alcohol was served. If you were carrying a concealed handgun and wanted to grab a bite to eat in a restaurant, you would have to leave your gun locked in your car. Not such a great idea since the gun could be stolen.

But in Massachusetts it was not legal to do it that way. In Massachusetts, a concealed handgun must be under your direct control (i.e., on your person) and cannot be left unattended and locked in your car. On the other hand, it is lawful to carry a concealed firearm in a place where alcohol is consumed. It was just the opposite in Virginia at that time. I had to make sure I remembered what state I was in so I would not be committing a crime.

Summary: The Need for a Universal State Permit

Today to exercise my constitutional right I need concealed-carry gun permits in Massachusetts, New Hampshire, Maine, and Connecticut because those are the states I generally travel in. But what would it cost me to be able to carry concealed legally in all fifty states?

First of all, it is not possible under current laws to carry in all fifty states because some states do not issue nonresident licenses. In other states, reciprocity or recognition might apply, but the actual expenses are not easily determined, though they would surely be in the thousands of dollars.

As previously mentioned, the costs include license application fees, fingerprinting, firearm safety certification courses, fees for police records and background checks, mailing costs, photographs, and other related expenses. In general, most state licenses are valid for four or five years and need to be renewed. Remember that the Massachusetts nonresident license is valid for only one year. The time and cost involved in doing the application paperwork is excessive.

As my story demonstrates, because of licensing requirements, it is very complicated, costly, and time-consuming to exercise my constitutional right to bear arms for self-defense. Would people tolerate such a restrictive process if there were such stringent requirements on the First Amendment right of freedom of religion? Would it be tolerable if you were required to pay $10,000 to state or local governments to practice your religion?

It is clear to me that existing state and federal laws do not enable one to bear arms for self-defense in many circumstances. The McClure-Volkmer Act at least makes it possible to get your firearms from State A to State B legally, but it does not allow you to do so in a way consistent with the Second Amendment right to bear arms for self-defense. A gun that's unloaded and locked in your car trunk is not useful for self-defense. Existing federal and state laws infringe upon your constitutional right to bear arms for self-defense.

From a GAO study of July 2012, I learned that Massachusetts had issued only one thousand nonresident permits; Maine, two thousand; and Connecticut, sixteen thousand. Either not many people are concerned about carrying concealed while visiting another state, or the paperwork and cost is too much trouble to bother with. A right not exercised is one that is more easily taken away without notice. In this day and age, with an increase in mass shootings and terrorist attacks, it is prudent to carry concealed firearms where it is permitted.

Proposed Changes in Federal and State Gun Laws

In this book I have recounted some examples of overly restrictive or ineffective gun laws that do not appear to be reducing gun violence in this country. I believe it is my duty as an US citizen to raise awareness and to offer some meaningful suggestions to changes in gun laws that may actually be beneficial to American society.

A Case for Universal Reciprocity

Here are my suggestions to federal and state lawmakers to revise gun laws to enable US citizens to exercise their constitutional right to carry firearms for self-defense. I consider my recommendations to be prudent given the increasing threat that people face from active shootings in the United States.

1. The US Congress should pass a *Constitutional Concealed Carry Reciprocity Act* that would allow law-abiding citizens who have concealed-carry permits in their resident states to travel into other states with their concealed handguns (just like driver's licenses). This would enable licensed holders to drive state to state without needing to get multiple gun licenses in order to carry concealed for self-defense purposes.

2. Laws prohibiting the carry of concealed firearms in *school zones* by licensed individuals should be revised. There is no reason why teachers and professors who are licensed and trained to carry concealed firearms should not be allowed to *voluntarily* carry concealed firearms in a school or university. In a lockdown situation, teachers and professors who are armed may be in a much better position to stop an active shooter than police who arrive too late.

3. Carrying a concealed firearm by a licensed individual into a *post office* (which is federal property) should no longer be prohibited. Someone out and about running errands should not be required to take their gun home before going into a post office to buy stamps or mail a package.

4. Carrying a concealed firearm by a licensed individual into a *bank* should not be prohibited by any state. Armed bank robberies occur very frequently nationwide, and an armed citizen with a concealed weapon may be in a position to save lives.

5. Laws that prohibit a licensed individual from carrying a concealed firearm into an establishment *where alcohol is served* should be repealed. Today's restaurants, and even local bars, are not Wild West places where drunks are shooting up the place.

6. Military personnel should be authorized to carry firearms concealed (or open carry) on *military bases* and facilities. If you can't trust our trained military personnel with firearms, then who can you trust?

7. All states should either be *"shall issue" or "no permit required"* with respect to the issuances of concealed carry permits. *"May issue"* discretion should be eliminated due to its arbitrary nature and inherent potential for abuse or discrimination (See *Peruta* case).

In closing, I must say that I understand the politics of Washington DC and many of the states and the intense emotions that gun violence elicits. Politicians frequently react in the immediate aftermath of mass gun shootings with new gun control proposals. However, it is my belief that good gun laws should be based upon objective reality and not irrational emotion and partisan politics.

I ask that you, the reader, be the judge on gun control, and if you favor any of my recommendations, write to your state and federal representatives and senators urging them to take action.

This book should also be read by any legislator involved in prescribing gun laws at the state or federal level. I have seen so many politicians and political pundits in the media talk about guns who have very little or incorrect knowledge about firearms. This book can be educational to them all.

In summary, the right to keep and bear arms for self-defense in the US is being infringed by the federal and state governments. Many gun laws are based on false premises that do not provide any increased public safety. To the contrary, some concealed carry restrictions may make the public less safe. It is time for sensible gun law reforms that actually do promote public safety and do not infringe on our right to bear arms for self-protection.

Appendix A

Terminology for Handguns and Ammunition

This appendix defines a variety of terms relating to handguns, ammunition, and concealed carry that one might encounter in general discussion. It is not intended to be a complete list but is offered as a basic reference. The terms described in this appendix have been derived from a variety of sources, including the books contained in the references, various handgun manuals, and gun manufacturer catalogs and glossaries. Definitions of various types of bullets can be found in chapter 3.

accessory rail: A feature on a semiauto handgun that accepts lights and sighting devices to aid the aiming process.

action: A series of moving parts that allows a firearm to be loaded, fired, and unloaded. See also *trigger*. Handgun triggers may be classified as single action or double action. See *striker-fire action*.

aimed shooting: The shooter uses sights to align the bore of the handgun with the line of sight to the target, as opposed to instinctive shooting or hip shooting.

ammunition: See chapters 3 and 4.

ballistic gelatin: A solid, colorless substance used as a testing medium to evaluate various types of ammunition. Gelatin is designed to simulate soft human tissue so it can be used for evaluating the effectiveness of firearms against humans. Typically, a bullet is fired into ballistic gelatin, and the penetration distance and other characteristics are scientifically evaluated. Gelatin is derived from collagen obtained from various animal by-products. (Note: For an excellent reference document, see the report *Ballistic Gelatin* by N. C. Nicholas and J. R. Welsch.)

bandoleer: A gun belt worn across the chest and fitted with small pockets or loops for carrying cartridges. For example, a leather shoulder ammunition belt.

biometric safe: A small, useful safe for storing handguns and small amounts of ammunition that prevents access by children or other unauthorized users. A biometric safe for handgun storage can be programmed with a user's fingerprints (e.g., thumb, index finger, etc.) to allow unlocking in seconds. A biometric safe is one way to comply with various state laws that require restricting access of handguns by unauthorized users while still enabling an authorized user ready access for a self-defense emergency.

bore: The inside of the barrel of a firearm.

bullet: A projectile, usually made of lead that is often covered with a layer of copper or other metal (see chapter 3).

cartridge: A complete round of ammunition consisting of a case, a bullet or projectile, the primer, and propellant powder. The case is a metal cylinder usually made of brass that is closed at one end and contains the other three components.

cartridge case: A metal cylinder, usually made of brass that is loaded at one end and contains the bullet, propellant powder, and primer. After the bullet has been fired, the case is often referred to as the "brass" that may be reloaded.

centerfire: A type of cartridge that has the primer centrally located in the base of the case. See *rimfire*.

center mass: The area to shoot on an assailant's body for maximum stopping power and effective incapacitation. The center mass area is shaped like the letter *T*, extending two to three inches wide across the forehead just above the eyes. The effective area runs down the center of the body to the lower stomach. In this zone lie the brain, the major blood vessels, the spine, and most of the vital organs.

chamber: The part of a firearm in which a cartridge is contained at the instant of firing.

clip: (1) A device that holds a set of cartridges that may be inserted into a magazine; (2) flat pieces of metal known as "moon clips" hold cartridges so they can be chambered and fired in revolvers specially designed for them. The term *clip* is often incorrectly used to refer to a magazine. A clip is not a magazine. See *magazine*.

compensated: A term used to describe handguns that have small holes bored into their gun barrel to vent the hot gases generated during firing. The purpose of venting is to reduce muzzle rise or felt recoil.

cylinder: The part of a revolver that holds ammunition in individual chambers that is rotated into firing position by the action of the trigger or hammer. Many revolvers have cylinders that hold either five, six, or even ten cartridges, such as smaller .22-caliber cartridges.

cylinder release latch: A part of many revolvers that releases the cylinder and allows it to swing out for loading and unloading.

decibel: Unit of noise measurement. Headgear used for ear protection at a shooting range is rated according to the level of protection (noise reduction) it provides, specified in decibels (dB). Noise levels are reduced approximately 20 to 30 dB.

discharge: To shoot or fire a weapon.

double action: A type of handgun action in which squeezing the trigger will both cock and release the hammer or internal firing mechanism. A double-action gun can be fired either by first cocking the hammer and then pulling the trigger, or by pulling the trigger without first cocking the hammer. In the case of revolvers, the double-action trigger pull also performs the function of rotating the next chamber to be fired into alignment with the firing pin.

double feed: A type of malfunction of a semiauto pistol that occurs when a round or expended case is in the chamber and a new round is fed up against it as if also trying to enter the chamber. It may be caused by a magazine with inadequate spring tension, allowing a round to inadvertently chamber during the slide's rearward movement, or because of failure to extract the spent cartridge. Upon the return forward motion of the slide, another round is stripped from the magazine and goes up against the case already in the chamber. See *tap-rack-bang*.

double tap: A double tap or "controlled pair" is a shooting technique where two well-aimed shots are fired at the same target with very little time between shots. The origin of the double-tap technique is credited to two British police chiefs in Shanghai during the 1930s who developed the method to overcome the limitations of full-metal-jacketed (FMJ) ammunition. If a double tap does not incapacitate an assailant, experts recommend a head shot because the assailant may be wearing body armor. This three-shot technique subsequently became known as the Mozambique, or Mogadishu shooting drill, but is commonly termed the failure-to-stop or triple-tap drill.

dry firing: Going through the action of cocking, aiming, and pulling the trigger on an unloaded gun. Dry firing can be helpful to learn the feel of a handgun, to practice sight alignment, or to check the operation of the gun. It is important to verify that the gun is empty before dry firing.

ejector: The part of a pistol that ejects an empty cartridge case or a cartridge from the gun.

extractor: A device that removes a fired case from a gun chamber.

felt recoil: The subjective recoil that is actually felt by the shooter, as opposed to the total recoil of the firearm as determined by mathematical calculation and physics.

field stripping: Disassembling a handgun to allow critical components to be cleaned and lubricated to ensure reliable operation of the handgun.

firing pin: A thin, pointed or rounded pin that strikes the primer or rim of a cartridge case to fire a bullet. The firing pin leaves an indentation in the primer or rim of the cartridge case.

firing pin block: A passive safety system that prevents a firing pin from going forward and striking the primer. This block is a safety system created to prevent an accidental discharge should the firearm be dropped.

flinching: An automatic human reflex caused by anticipating the recoil of a firearm.

gilding metal: A metal alloy of copper and zinc used as a bullet jacket.

grain: The unit of weight generally used to specify the weight of bullets or propellant powder. One ounce equals 437.5 grains. For example, a 230-grain .45-caliber cartridge has a bullet that weighs 230 grains.

grip: (1) the manner of placing one's hand(s) upon the handgun to allow its control and accurate firing, (2) the handle on a handgun.[17]

grooves: The shallow, spiral cuts in a bore that together with the lands make up the rifling in the bore of a barrel. See *rifling* and *land*.

---

17. Lenny Magill (a concealed carry expert) recommends a one-handed grip for self-defense because it exposes less of the torso to an assailant who might be shooting back. A shooter's vulnerable target area is nearly twice as wide (twenty inches) with a standard two-hand grip as compared to a one-hand grip (eleven inches). In essence, you are presenting a smaller target to an aggressor by using a one-handed grip, thereby reducing that aggressor's chances of hitting you. Nevertheless, you also reduce the probability of hitting the aggressor.

hammer: A part of the action of a handgun that, when activated by the trigger, drives the firing pin against the primer, igniting the powder and firing the gun.

handgun: A firearm that has a short stock and is designed to be held, aimed, and fired with one hand. The term *handgun* is used synonymously with *pistol* throughout this book. The two most common types of handguns in use today are the revolver and the semiautomatic (also known as autoloader).

hangfire: A noticeable delay in the ignition of a cartridge after the primer has been struck by the firing pin, after which a bullet may be discharged from the gun. With a hangfire, the shooter pulls the trigger but no shot goes off immediately. A hangfire may be caused by deteriorated or contaminated ammunition.

high-angle jam: A type of malfunction in a semiauto handgun, when after firing a cartridge it stops halfway out of the magazine and remains stuck halfway in the chamber held there at a forty-five-degree angle. Known to occur with jacketed truncated cone (JTC) bullets.

holster: Handgun accessory that allows an individual to carry a firearm on one's person, whether concealed or open carry. There are many different varieties of holsters on the market. Two useful types of holsters for concealed carry of a handgun are (1) an inside-waistband (IWB) holster and (2) a Miami Classic shoulder holster. Recommended reading: *Holsters for Combat and Concealed Carry* by R. K. Campbell (Paladin Press).

inside-waistband (IWB) holster: A holster useful for concealed carry that attaches to a belt and allows a person to carry a handgun close to the body and inside the belt where it cannot be seen.

instinctive shooting: The shooter looks at the target, rather than the front sight of the handgun, and relies upon natural pointing ability to align the bore of the handgun with the target. The shooter takes aim at the target by pointing the gun as you would point your index finger at the spot you want to hit, without using the conventional sight picture.

160

internal lock: A feature of a handgun that can be used to lock a manual safety in the "on" position. This lock will prevent the use of the gun by anyone who does not have the key or other device to unlock it.

jacket: The metal covering a bullet's core, usually copper, steel, or other metal. Most cores are lead, although there are frangible (fragmented) cores made of other metals or materials.

jam: A malfunction of a firearm that prevents the action from operating. A jam may be caused by faulty parts or ammunition, improper maintenance, or improper use of the firearm, such as limp wristing.

kick: A subjective term for the recoil felt by a handgun shooter.

land: The raised area of the bore in a rifled barrel that is between the grooves.

large-capacity ammunition-feeding device: A magazine, belt, drum, feed strip, or similar device manufactured after the date of enactment of the Violent Crime Control and Law Enforcement Act of 1994 that has a capacity of, or that can be readily restored or converted to accept, more than ten rounds of ammunition (18 U.S.C. § 921).

limp-wristing malfunction: A semiautomatic handgun malfunction caused by improper grip of the firearm. If a semiautomatic pistol is not held correctly with a firm wrist, recoil after the gun is fired can cause the slide to not cycle properly. As a result, a cartridge can jam as it moves from the magazine to the chamber, or a spent cartridge casing can fail to eject.

live round: A round that contains a primer, a powder charge, and a bullet in a case that is ready to be fired.

loaded chamber indicator: A small part that protrudes from the top or the side of the slide of a semiauto handgun and provides a visual indication when a cartridge is present in the firing chamber. Also called a load indicator.

magazine: A cartridge holder for storing ammunition that feeds the ammunition into the firearm's chamber for firing. In a magazine, a spring pushes cartridges into position that are then fed into the firing chamber by operation of the action of the handgun. Generally, there are two types of magazines for semiautomatic handguns: (1) single stack and (2) double stack.

- A single-stack magazine holds one round of ammunition on top of another, is narrower than a double-stack magazine, and holds fewer rounds. It has the advantage of enabling a grip that fits smaller hands.

- A double-stack magazine staggers the rounds of ammunition so that it can hold more rounds for a given length.

For example, the .45-caliber Glock Model 36 has a single-stack magazine that holds six rounds of ammunition, while the .45-caliber Glock Model 37 has a double-stack magazine that holds ten rounds of ammunition.

magazine capacity: The maximum number of rounds or bullets that a magazine of a specific firearm can hold. Magazines that have the capacity to hold more than ten rounds are generally considered to be large-capacity or high-capacity magazines.[18]

magazine loader: A small metal or plastic part that fits over a handgun magazine and compresses the magazine spring, making it easier to load cartridges into the magazine. Magazine loaders take the place of your thumb and are sometimes referred to as *thumb savers*.

---

18. Six states and the District of Columbia currently ban or restrict large-capacity magazines. Maryland defines a large-capacity magazine as a magazine capable of accepting more than twenty rounds. New Jersey defines it as one capable of accepting more than fifteen rounds. California, Hawaii, Massachusetts, and DC define it as a magazine capable of accepting more than ten rounds. New York defines high-capacity magazines as magazines capable of holding more than seven rounds. (See "magazine.")

magazine release: A latch that releases the magazine so that it can be removed from the handgun.

magazine safety: A handgun safety device that prevents the firing of a semiautomatic handgun unless a magazine is in place.

magazine safety disconnect: A feature on a semiauto handgun designed to prevent the gun from being fired when the magazine is removed, even if a live round remains in the firing chamber.

malfunctions (semiauto handgun): Failure to feed, fire, or eject a round; failure to accept or eject a magazine; or failure of the slide to remain open after the last round has been fired (if the handgun is designed to do so). In general, three types of malfunctions are (1) failure to fire, (2) failure to eject, and (3) double feed. Failure to fire may be due to a magazine that is not fully seated, defective ammunition, or a result of a light strike to the primer. Failure to eject, also referred to as a *stovepipe*, occurs when an expended cartridge case gets wedged between the slide and the chamber. Failure to eject may be caused by a damaged extractor or ejector, or due to shooter error known as limp-wristing. See *double-feed*.

Miami Classic shoulder holster: One of the world's most recognized holsters popularized by actor Don Johnson on *Miami Vice*. It is a favorite holster of law enforcement and security personnel. The holster includes a harness and magazine carrier and can be used effectively for concealed carry under a suit jacket or coat.

misfire: Failure of an ammunition cartridge to fire after the firing pin contacts the primer. The bullet does not separate from the cartridge. If after pulling the trigger a shooter hears a click and no shot is heard, the shooter should wait at least thirty seconds with the gun still pointed in a safe direction to make sure a delayed discharge does not occur.

mouse gun: A small revolver or semiautomatic handgun intended for self-defense, of .380 ACP (9 mm short) caliber or less. Typical calibers include .32 ACP and .22 long rifle.
(*Gun Digest* 2013, 102–113)

mushrooming: The act of expansion of a bullet upon impact with a target, usually associated with a soft-point or hollow-point bullet.

muzzle: The front end of the barrel from which a projectile or bullet exits.

muzzle flash: Fire created from the burning of excess propellant that follows the bullet out of a muzzle and produces a bright flash that can temporarily blind a shooter at nighttime or identify the shooter's location.

muzzle rise: Barrel lift upon shooting that affects the next shot because the sights are not on the target after barrel lift occurs.

octagonal rifling: A type of rifling in Glock pistols that decreases bullet deformation and increases accuracy and velocity due to the improved seal in the barrel. There are only lands but not grooves in octagonal rifling, a variation of polygonal rifling.

open carry: Carrying a firearm in public, such as in a holster, where it is in plain sight, as opposed to concealed carry where it cannot be seen. Open-carry laws vary from state to state.[19]

out-of-battery: Refers to the status of a weapon before the action has returned to the normal firing position. The slide of a semiauto handgun may not return to its proper position after firing, and the handgun may not fire when it is out-of-battery.

packing heat: Slang term for carrying a concealed handgun, whether legally or illegally.

piece: Slang term for a handgun.

pistol: A gun that has a short barrel and can be held, aimed, and fired with one hand. The term *pistol* is used synonymously with

---

19. My personal viewpoint is that unless you are in some remote rural town where it is legal and commonplace to walk around with a firearm on your hip, or you are a law enforcement official, it is probably not a good idea to open carry even in a state where it is legal to do so. Some people get uneasy seeing firearms openly visible. Unpleasant run-ins with law enforcement and frightened people have been known to occur, and you might even be charged with disturbing the peace.

handgun in this book. Pistols may be single shot, semiautomatic, or fully automatic.

plinking: Random shooting at a variety of targets for the fun of it. Plinking with a .22-caliber pistol is common because .22-caliber ammunition is relatively inexpensive and readily available.

pocket pistol: Any small, easily concealable self-defense handgun intended for protection at very close range. Typical pocket pistol calibers are .22, .25 ACP, .32 ACP, or .380 ACP.

polygonal rifling: The rifling inside the barrel has a polygon shape and provides a better bullet-to-barrel seal with jacketed ammunition, resulting in higher velocity compared to conventionally rifled barrels of the same length. Polygonal rifling is reported to increase projectile velocities from thirty to fifty feet per second, which also results in a significant gain in energy for a handgun bullet. See *octagonal rifling*.

porting: Small holes manufactured or machined (commonly by spark discharge machining) into a gun barrel near the muzzle that vent the hot gases generated during firing. Ports can reduce felt recoil and muzzle rise. See also *compensated*.

powder charge: A fast-burning chemical compound used as a propellant, generally contained inside the body of a cartridge case.

primer: A chemical compound sensitive to impact used for igniting the propellant powder in a cartridge case. The striking of the primer by a hammer or a firing pin ignites the primer, which in turn ignites the powder that fires the bullet. It can also refer to the component of a cartridge case that contains the primer compound, as in the primer of a center-fire cartridge.

printing: In concealed carry, pistol printing refers to the impression made by a concealed handgun onto a garment of clothing worn by a concealer that reveals that a gun is "concealed." Clothing and holsters for concealed carry should be selected so as to avoid printing.

propellant: A fast-burning chemical compound that is ignited, causing a bullet to be fired. Propellant generally contains its own oxidizer and does not depend on the atmosphere for an oxidizer such as oxygen.

quick draw: To draw a handgun from a concealed holster quickly, Lenny Magill recommends a four-step process that can be performed in about one second with practice as follows: (1) clear the clothing for access to the concealed handgun, (2) move your hand to the gun, (3) acquire a firm grip on the gun, and (4) point the gun at the target and fire the weapon.

rack: To pull the slide of a semiauto pistol backward and then release it to chamber the first round.

receiver: The frame upon which the slide is attached and the magazine is inserted.

recoil: The backward force of a firearm upon firing. See *felt recoil*.

rifling: The surface geometry inside a barrel that makes the projectile/bullet spin as it leaves the barrel, stabilizing the bullet in flight and improving accuracy. Rifling is commonly lands and grooves, but see also *polygonal rifling*.

rimfire: A rimfire cartridge has the chemical compound of the primer located inside the rim of the cartridge case. See *centerfire*.

round: Another term for a cartridge.

safety: A design feature that is intended to prevent inadvertent firing of a handgun by either blocking or disconnecting the firing mechanism. A safety can be either active (requiring activation by the user) or passive. A handgun can have single or multiple safeties. Example: Glock handguns have three safeties: (1) trigger safety, (2) firing pin safety, and (3) drop safety.[20]

---

20. One person's safety might be another person's hazard. When Glock pistols were first under development, external safety levers were considered since many existing handguns had them. However, Glock found that many soldiers and police forgot whether their manual safeties were on or off, which led to confusion and accidental discharges. Many experts claimed safety levers could be a potential source of mishandling

Saturday night special: Slang expression for an inexpensive, commonly used handgun.

sear: The catch in a gunlock that holds the hammer in a half-cocked or fully cocked position.

semi-automatic: Capable of using some of the energy of a firing cartridge to extract the case and chamber the next round, and requiring a separate pull of the trigger to fire each round.

semiautomatic handgun: A type of handgun that fires a single cartridge each time the trigger is pulled, and automatically extracts and ejects the empty case and inserts a new cartridge into the chamber. Semiautomatic handguns have several advantages over revolvers as concealed-carry weapons. Generally, semiautos are easier to conceal, more comfortable to wear due to their slimness, can be reloaded more quickly, and have larger ammunition capacity.

sidearm: A pistol carried at the side or waist.

sights: Mechanical, optical, or electronic devices used to aim a pistol.

- Front sight. Located on the front end of the muzzle or slide.

- Rear sight. Located at the rear of the barrel or slide.

- Tritium sights. Tritium is a radioactive element (an isotope of hydrogen) that glows in the dark and is used on the front and rear sights of handguns to aid in seeing at night.

- Laser sight. Some handguns may be equipped with a laser that transmits a bright ray of light that marks the target. Sights are available with rays in visible red or green as well as infrared for use with night-vision equipment. (The acronym LASER stands for *light amplification by stimulated emission of radiation*)

---

and could be hazardous or a hindrance to the quick operation of a handgun. (Barrett 2013) sight alignment: One of the most important factors to firing an accurate shot. Proper alignment of the two sights means that the top of the front sight is even with the top of the rear sight. The front sight must also be centered in the notch of the rear sight so that there is an equal amount of space on each side of the front sight.

silencer: A sound suppressor device designed to reduce the noise, by any amount, of a semiautomatic handgun upon firing. The smaller the bore size of the weapon, the easier it is to silence. Revolvers, generally, cannot be silenced by a sound suppressor. In Massachusetts per M.G.L. chapter 269 section 10A, possession of a silencer is a felony punishable by up to five years in a state prison.

single action: A type of handgun action in which pulling the trigger will release the hammer. Single action describes a gun in which the hammer must be cocked manually, or in the case of a semiauto, by action of the slide, before it can be fired. In a single-action gun, pulling the trigger performs only the single action of dropping the hammer to fire the gun. Pulling the trigger does *not* perform the double action of cocking the hammer and then dropping it.

slide: The part of a self-loading handgun that contains the firing pin and the extractor. Its movement back and forth cocks the gun, chambers another cartridge for firing, and ejects the spent cartridge. The slide rests on top of the receiver or frame.

slide lock: The part of a semiautomatic handgun that is designed to hold the slide of the handgun to the rear position and then release it to move forward. The slide lock is also activated automatically when the last shot is fired (if a magazine is in the gun), or it can be manually operated. Also known as *slide release* or *slide stop*.

small arms: Handguns of .50 caliber (12.7 mm) or less.

snubnose: A short-barreled revolver, typically characterized by a double-action trigger mechanism, a swing-out cylinder, a small frame, and a two-inch barrel.

SOB (small of back): The center of a small recess on a person's back that curves slightly inward and where a subcompact pistol can be comfortably concealed. With an appropriate SOB holster, a handgun may be concealed by a light jacket or with shirttails out. The gun will be completely out of sight and relatively easy to access.

speedloader: An ammunition holder that enables a user to quickly and simultaneously reload cartridges into all chambers in a revolver cylinder.

squib load: A cartridge that develops less than normal pressure or velocity after ignition of the cartridge. The bullet may exit the barrel at a significantly reduced speed or get stuck in the barrel. A squib load may be caused by deteriorated or contaminated ammunition or an insufficient amount of powder in the cartridge.

stance: The positioning of the body of a shooter when firing a handgun. Four types of shooting stances are as follows:

- Weaver stance. A right-handed shooter faces the target with feet shoulder width apart, with the left foot forward of the right, angling the chest slightly away from the target.

- Isosceles stance. Shooter faces straight forward to the target with feet shoulder width apart. The shooter's two legs form an isosceles triangle with the ground.

- Fairbairn stance. Instinctive point shooting from a crouched position without the use of conventional sights.

- One-handed sideways stance. Using a one-handed grip, a right-handed shooter stands sideways with the right leg in front of the left, presenting a smaller target to an aggressor.

stovepipe: A malfunction in a semiautomatic handgun in which a fired cartridge is not ejected completely but gets stuck vertically in the ejection port, resembling a stovepipe.

striker-fire action: Refers to a type of pistol action that employs an internal striker mechanism to detonate the primer. In operation, the pistol is normally in a partially cocked condition. Pulling the trigger releases the striker mechanism to fire the pistol.

tap-rack-bang: A method used to clear a handgun that won't fire due to a stoppage malfunction. To remedy the first step is to tap the magazine floorplate upward into the magazine well to ensure it is properly seated. The next step is to rack or cycle the action. Third, the pistol is fired in a safe direction.

target shooting: Shooting at inanimate objects, such as paper targets or cans, for practice to improve accuracy, for competitive shooting matches, in safety courses to demonstrate competency in handling a firearm, or for proficiency to be able to respond quickly to a self-defense situation.[21]

trajectory: The path of a bullet from the handgun to the target. If a bullet travels over a long distance, the effects of gravity on the bullet must be considered for an accurate hit. For a self-defense situation, the target is usually so close that the effects of gravity are not a consideration.

trigger: The lever pressed by the finger of a shooter to fire a bullet from a handgun. The trigger is located on the underside of the handgun frame. Triggers may be classified as single action or double action.

---

21. For self-defense proficiency, Lenny Magill recommends practicing concealed-carry draws from a holster and firing at a paper plate (eight inches in diameter) from a distance of seven feet. Statistically, approximately 80 percent of gunfights occur at this close range. Distances of twelve feet and twenty-one feet are also recommended for practice. The distance of twenty-one feet is considered the maximum needed for practice. In a legal defense, beyond that distance the question could arise whether one should have fled, took cover, or otherwise avoided confrontation and serious injury or death. Being able to consistently hit an eight-inch paper plate from distances of seven, twelve, and twenty-one feet is considered accurate enough for self-defense target shooting. (Magill 1996)

trigger guard: The part of the handgun located on the underside of the frame designed to protect the trigger and to reduce the possibility of an unintentional firing.

trigger lock: A passive safety system that interrupts the rearward travel of the trigger, which prevents a discharge when a firearm is dropped. This system is disengaged when the trigger is pulled to the rear.

trigger lock (key activated): A device that, when locked in place by means of a key, prevents a potential user from pulling the trigger of the handgun without first removing the trigger lock by use of the key. A trigger lock is not to be confused with a manual trigger safety that must be moved, turned, or otherwise activated to physically enable the trigger to be pulled to the rear.

trigger pull: Refers to the amount of force that must be applied to a trigger to cause the handgun to fire. For example, standard Glock pistols generally require about 5.5 pounds of force to pull the trigger.

trigger squeeze: Movement of the trigger finger in applying increasing pressure on the trigger straight to the rear without disturbing sight alignment until the handgun fires.

twist: Characteristic of rifling in a barrel expressed as a number of turns per inch or centimeter.

wheel gun: Another name for a revolver.

Acronyms

ACP	Automatic Colt Pistol
AP	armor piercing
BLD	*Black's Law Dictionary*
CCW	carry concealed weapons
DPX	Deep Penetrating X-Panding
FBI	Federal Bureau of Investigation
FMJ	full metal jacket
FOPA	Firearms Owners' Protection Act
GAP	Glock Automatic Pistol
IWB	inside-the-waist band
JHP	jacketed hollow point
JSP	jacketed soft point
JTC	jacketed truncated cone
LCP	lightweight compact pistol
LCR	lightweight compact revolver
LR	long rifle
LTC	license to carry
MC	metal-cased or metal-clad
MGL	Massachusetts General Law
MRSA	Maine Revised Statutes Annotated
NICS	National Instant Criminal Background Check System
NIJ	National Institute of Justice
+P	plus P
+P+	plus P plus
PPK	Polizei Pistole Kriminalmodell
RII	relative incapacitation index
RNL	round-nose lead
RSP	relative stopping power
SAFE	Secure Ammunition and Firearms Enforcement
SJHP	semijacketed hollow point
SJSP	semijacketed soft point
SOB	small-of-the-back
SST	super shock tip
STHP	silver-tipped hollow point
S&W	Smith & Wesson

SWC	semiwadcutter
TKOF	Taylor Knock-Out Factor
U.S.C.	*United States Code*
U.S.C.A.	*United States Code Annotated*
WC	wadcutter
WMR	Winchester Magnum Rimfire
XD	X-treme Duty

Appendix B

Firearms Safety

National Rifle Association Gun Safety Rules

1. Always keep the gun pointed in a safe direction.
2. Always keep your finger off the trigger until ready to shoot.
3. Always keep the gun unloaded until ready to use.

These three fundamental gun safety rules were posted at the NRA shooting range in Fairfax, Virginia when I used to go shooting there.

Glock Rules of Firearm Safety

There are a few other rules that are wise to practice. The basic rules of firearms safety according to Glock are as follows:

1. Handle all firearms as if they were loaded.
2. Always keep the firearm pointed in a safe direction.
3. Keep your finger out of the gun's trigger guard and off the trigger until you have aligned the gun's sights on a safe target and you have made the decision to fire.
4. Always be certain that your target and the surrounding area are safe before firing.
5. Whenever you handle a firearm, the first thing you should do (while keeping it pointed in a safe direction with your finger outside the trigger guard) is to open the action to determine whether or not the firearm is loaded.
6. Thoroughly read the instruction manual supplied with your firearm.

7. Before firing your weapon, you should routinely make sure that your firearm is in good working order and that the barrel is clear of dirt and obstructions.
8. Only use ammunition recommended by the firearm manufacturer, and always be certain that the ammunition matches the caliber of your gun.
9. Quality ear and eye protection should always be worn when shooting or observing.
10. Never use firearms while under the influence of drugs or alcohol.
11. All firearms should be stored unloaded and secured in a safe storage case inaccessible to children and untrained adults.
12. The transportation of firearms is regulated by federal, state, and local laws. Always transport your firearm in a safe, unloaded condition and in accordance with applicable laws. (Author: One exception is if you are carrying concealed your gun will be loaded.)

(*Source:* Glock 2005. *The Basic Rules of Firearm Safety.* Reprinted with permission.)

References

Adams, Les. 1996. *The Second Amendment Primer: A Citizen's Guidebook to the History, Sources, and Authorities for the Constitutional Guarantee of the Right to Keep and Bear Arms.* Birmingham, Alabama: Palladium Press.

Adams, Ronald J., Thomas M. McTernan, and Charles Remsberg. 1980. *Street Survival: Tactics for Armed Encounters.* Northbrook, Illinois: Calibre Press.

Anderson, W. French. 2006. *Forensic Analysis of the April 11, 1986, FBI Firefight.* Boulder, Colorado: Paladin Press.

Ayoob, Massad. 2012. *Gun Digest Book of Concealed Carry.* 2nd ed. Iola, Wisconsin: Krause.

Barnes, Frank C. 2006. *Cartridges of the World.* 11th ed. Iola, Wisconsin: Gun Digest Books.

Barrett, Paul M. 2013. *Glock: The Rise of America's Gun.* New York: Broadway Paperbacks, Random House.

Bird, Chris. 2004. *The Concealed Handgun Manual: How to Choose, Carry, and Shoot a Gun in Self-Defense.* San Antonio, Texas: Privateer Publications.

Bird, Chris. 2007. *Thank God I Had a Gun: True Accounts of Self-Defense.* San Antonio, Texas: Privateer Publications.

Blair, J. Pete, and Katherine W. Schweit. 2014. A Study of Active Shooter Incidents in the United States Between 2000 and 2013. Texas State University and Federal Bureau of Investigation, US Department of Justice, Washington, DC.

References

Boatman, Robert H. 2002. *Living with Glocks: The Complete Guide to the New Standard in Combat Handguns*. Boulder, Colorado: Paladin Press.

Branca, Andrew F. 2013. *The Law of Self-Defense: The Indispensable Guide for the Armed Citizen*. Maynard, Massachusetts: Law of Self-Defense.

Bussard, Michael E., and Stanton L. Wormley Jr. 2010. *NRA Firearms Sourcebook: Your Ultimate Guide to Guns, Ballistics and Shooting*. Third Printing. Fairfax, Virginia: National Rifle Association.

Casada, Jim. 2010. *The Experts' Guide to Handgun Marksmanship for Self-Defense, Target Shooting, Hunting*. Birmingham, Alabama: Palladium Press.

Chiaramonte, Perry. 2014, January 26. "Gun Flight: Smith & Wesson, Ruger Quit California Over Stamping Requirement," Fox News.com.

Chin, Paula. 1991, November 4. "A Texas Massacre." *People Weekly Magazine*, Vol. 36 No. 17.

Connecticut Department of Public Safety. 2002. "General Statutes of Connecticut" (Revised to October 1, 2002).

Copeland, Larry and Doug Richards. 2014, April 23. "Ga. Governor Signs 'Guns Everywhere' into Law," *USA Today*.

Cruz, Jennifer and Joshua Rhett Miller. 2014, July 16. Guns.com, Fox News.

Dubner, Stephen J. and Steven Levitt. 2005. *Freakonomics: A Rogue Economist Explores the Hidden Side of Everything*. New York: William Morrow and Company.

References

Fitzpatrick, Brad. 2013. *Shooter's Bible Guide to Concealed Carry.* New York: Skyhorse.

Fletcher, George P. 1988. *A Crime of Self Defense: Bernard Goetz and the Law on Trial.* Chicago: University of Chicago Press.

Florida Department of Agriculture and Consumer Services (Division of Licensing). 2008. "Concealed Weapon or Firearm License Application Instructions and Chapter 790, Florida Statutes" (Revision July 2008).

Florida Department of Agriculture and Consumer Services (Division of Licensing) 2005, 2012. "Questions and Answers Pertaining to the Use of Deadly Force for Lawful Self-Defense" (Revisions October 2005 and April 2012).

Forker, Bob. 2013. *Ammo and Ballistics for Hunters, Shooters, and Collectors.* 5th ed. Long Beach, California: Safari Press.

Garner, Bryan A., editor. 2009. *Black's Law Dictionary.* 9th ed. St. Paul, Minnesota: Thomson Reuters.

Glidden, Ronald C., and John M. Collins. 2013. *Law Enforcement Guide to Firearms Law.* 21st ed. South Grafton, Massachusetts: Municipal Police Institute, in cooperation with Glidden Training and Consulting.

Glock. 2005. *The Basic Rules of Firearm Safety.* Smyrna, Georgia: Glock.

Glock. 2016. *Annual 2016 Buyer's Guide.* New York: Harris.

Grace, Melissa. 2012, March 19. "Tennessee Tourist Who Brought Gun to 9/11 Memorial Gets Misdemeanor Plea Deal." *New York Daily News.*

References

Greenfield Recorder, "Vermont Man Arrested on Guns, Ammo Charges," April 6, 2013.

Hartnik, A. E. 2002. *The Complete Encyclopedia of Pistols and Revolvers*. Edison, New Jersey: Chartwell Books.

Hawkins, Awr. 2015, November 23. "Teachers Carrying Guns in 40 Ohio Schools," Breitbart.

Hawkins, Awr. 2016, March 6. "Eight States Where the 2nd Amendment Is Your Concealed Carry Permit," Breitbart. http://www.breitbart.com/big-government/2016/03/06/eight-states-where-2nd-amendment-is-only-carry-permit-required/

Hayden, Jen. 2015, October 20. "Utah Teachers Are Allowed to Carry Concealed Guns, Parents Are Not Allowed to Find Out Who's Carrying." *Daily Kos*.

Holbrook, Stephen P. 2000. "Nazi Firearms Laws and the Disarming of the German Jews." *Arizona Journal of International and Comparative Law* 17 (3): 485–535.

Johnston, Danny. 2013, July 30. "Arkansas School to Arm Teachers with Concealed Weapons," The Associated Press, *New York Daily News*.

Jones, Ashby. 2013, September 12. "Gun Rights Supporters Score Big Win in Colorado Recalls," *Wall Street Journal*.

Kahr Arms. 2016. *All American*, 16th ed., Worcester, Massachusetts: Kahr Arms.

Kalil, Joe, K. L. Jamison, and R. K. Campbell. 2013. *Concealed Carry Legal Defense: After You Defend Your Life, Be Prepared to Defend Your Freedom*. Lexington, Kentucky: United States Concealed Carry Association and Delta Media.

Kappas, J. Scott. 2013. *Traveler's Guide to the Firearm Laws of the Fifty States.* 17th ed. Kovington, Kentucky: Traveler's Guide.

Kasler, Peter Alan. 1992. *Glock: The New Wave in Combat Handguns.* Boulder, Colorado: Paladin Press.

Keith, Elmer. (1961) 2013. *Six Guns: The Standard Reference Work.* Reprint. Lexington, Kentucky: Sportsman's Vintage Press.

Kelly, Larry, and J. D. Jones. 1990. *Hunting for Handgunners.* Northbrook, Illinois: DBI Books.

Kimber. 2016. *Lands and Grooves,* New York: Outdoor Sportsmen Group.

Kopel, David. 2014, February 13. "Ninth Circuit Strikes California's Restrictive Rule Against Licensed Carry of Handguns." *The Washington Post.*

Korwin, Alan, and Michael P. Anthony. 1999. *Gun Laws of America.* Phoenix, Arizona: Bloomfield Press.

Korwin, Alan, and Steve Maniscako. 2001. *The Virginia Gun Owner's Guide.* Phoenix, Arizona: Bloomfield Press.

Korwin, Alan, David B. Kopel, and Stephen P. Holbrook. 2004. *Supreme Court Gun Cases.* Phoenix, Arizona: Bloomfield Press.

Kyle, Chris. 2013. *American Gun: A History of the US in Ten Firearms.* New York: Harper Collins.

LaPierre, Wayne. 2003. *Guns, Freedom and Terrorism.* Nashville, Tennessee: WND Books.

Lee, Jerry, ed. 2014. *Gun Digest 2015.* 69th ed. Iola, Wisconsin: Krause Publications.

References

Lieb, David A. 2013, September 12. "Missouri Legislature Closer to Veto That Would Lessen Fed Gun Control," Associated Press, *Greenfield Recorder*.

Long, Duncan. 1996. *Glock's Handguns*. El Dorado, Arkansas: Desert Publications.

Lott, John R. Jr. 2003. *The Bias Against Guns: Why Almost Everything You've Heard About Gun Control Laws Is Wrong*. Washington, DC: Regnery.

Magill, Lenny. 1996. *Concealed Carry: Tips, Techniques and Secrets of the Pros*. San Diego, California: Lenny Magill Productions.

Maine State Police. 2009. "State of Maine LAWS Relating to Permits to Carry Concealed Firearms."

Mann, Richard. 2013. *American Rifleman Magazine*. "The .22 Magnum for Self-Defense?" June, 52–57.

Marshall, Evan P., and Edwin J. Sanow. 2001. *Stopping Power: A Practical Analysis of the Latest Handgun Ammunition*. Boulder, Colorado: Paladin Press.

McLeod, Terrence. 2001. *Concealed Pocket Pistols: How to Choose and Use Small-Caliber Handguns*. Boulder, Colorado: Paladin Press.

Miller, Emily. 2013. *Emily Gets Her Gun...but Obama Wants to Take Yours*. Washington, DC: Regnery.

Mooar, Brian. 1992, March 30. "Jack Ruby's Gun Seized in Encounter at Capitol." *The Washington Post*.

Millward, Wade and Carmen Forman. 2014, September 1. *News 21*, Arizona State University: Walter Cronkite School of Journalism and Mass Communication.

References

Napolitano, Andrew P. 2010. *Lies the Government Told You.* Nashville, Tennessee: Thomas Nelson.

National Firearms Museum. 2002. *Real Guns of Reel Heroes.* Fairfax, Virginia.

National Rifle Association. 1988. *The Basics of Personal Protection: A Practical Handgun Handbook.* Fairfax, Virginia.

National Rifle Association. 1991. *The Basics of Pistol Shooting.* Fairfax, Virginia.

National Rifle Association. 1989. *NRA Firearms Fact Book.* 3rd ed. Fairfax, Virginia.

National Rifle Association. 2000. *NRA Guide to the Basics of Personal Protection in the Home.* Fairfax, Virginia.

Nicholas, N. C., and J. R. Welsch. 2004, February. *Ballistic Gelatin.* Institute for Non-Lethal Defense Technologies Report, Applied Research Laboratory, Pennsylvania State University.

Nugent, Ted. 2001. *God, Guns and Rock 'n' Roll.* Washington, DC: Regnery.

Olivier, Alfred G., and Arthur J. Dziemian. 1965, March. "Wound Ballistics of 6.5 mm Mannlicher Carcano Ammunition." Edgewood Arsenal, Maryland: US Army Chemical Research and Development Laboratories (CRDLR 3264).

Peruta, Edward v. County of San Diego, Case Number 10-56971 (June 16, 2015).

Prasac, Max. 2013. *Gun Digest Book of RUGER Revolvers: The Definitive History.* Iola, Wisconsin: Krause.

PTOOMA Productions. 2004. *The Complete Glock Reference Guide.*

References

Rinker, Robert A. 2002. *Understanding Firearm Ballistics*. USA: Mulberry House.

SIG Sauer. 2016. *When It Counts*. Newington, New Hampshire: SIG Sauer.

Sommers, Michael A. 2001. *The Right to Bear Arms*. 1st ed. New York: Rosen Publishing Group.

Supica, Jim, and Richard Nahas. 2006. *Standard Catalog of Smith and Wesson*. Iola, Wisconsin: Gun Digest Books.

Sweeney, Patrick. 2003. *Glock: A Comprehensive Review (Design, History, Use)*. Iola, Wisconsin: Krause.

Taurus. 2013. *Carry On*. New York: Intermedia Outdoors.

Taylor, Chuck. 1997. *Combat Handgunnery*. 4th ed. Iola, Wisconsin: Krause.

Texas Concealed Handgun Laws and Selected Statutes. 2011–2012. Austin: Texas Department of Public Safety.

Thomas, Duane. 1997. *The Truth About Handguns: Exploding the Myths, Hype, and Misinformation*. Boulder, Colorado: Paladin Press.

Tueller, Dennis. 1983. "How Close Is Too Close?" SWAT Magazine.

U.S. Congress. Senate. 2015. "Constitutional Concealed Carry Reciprocity Act of 2015." 114th Congress.

U.S. Department of Justice, National Institute of Justice. 2001, June. NIJ Standard -0101.04 "Ballistic Resistance of Personal Body Armor." Washington, DC.

References

U.S. Department of Justice, Bureau of Alcohol, Tobacco, Firearms and Explosives. 2012, April. "Form 4473 (5300.9) Firearms Transaction Record Part I—Over-the Counter."

U.S. General Accountability Office. 2012. July 17. "Gun Control States' Laws and Requirements for Concealed Carry Permits Vary Across the Nation."

U.S. Supreme Court. 1895. *Beard v. United States*, 158 U.S. 550.

U.S. Supreme Court. 2008. *District of Columbia v. Heller*, 554 U.S. 570.

U.S. Supreme Court. 2010. *McDonald v. City of Chicago*, 561 U.S. 742.

Vilos, Mitch, and Evan Vilos. 2010. *Self-Defense Laws of All 50 States*. Centreville, Utah: Guns West.

Walther. *Product Catalog, Built For Life*. Fort Smith, Arkansas: Walther Arms, 2016.

Waters, Robert A. *The Best Defense: True Stories of Intended Victims Who Defended Themselves with a Firearm*. Nashville, Tennessee: Cumberland House.

Whitley, John E. 2014, July 9. *Concealed Carry Permit Holders Across the United States*. Report from the Crime Prevention Research Center. *http://crimeresearch.org/wp-content/uploads/2014/07/Concealed-Carry-Permit-Holders-Across-the-United-States.pdf*

Wilson, R. L. 2007. *Ruger & His Guns: A History of the Man, the Company, and Their Firearms*. New York: Chartwell Books.

Alphabetical Index

Acknowledgements

Some legal definitions in this book have been reprinted from *Black's Law Dictionary* with permission of the publisher, Thomson Reuters. These definitions are identified as such by the citation (BLD) after the definition.

Glock, Inc. (Smyrna, GA) for granting permission to reprint their *Basic Rules of Firearms Safety*.

Mr. Gregory E. Saunders, Mr. John Binford, and Mr. Gary Kwitkoski (who were all professional colleagues of mine at the Pentagon) for their editorial review.

Mr. Michael Thomas (retired Police Officer, Leverett, MA) for suggesting some useful reference books.

Ms. Donna Duvall, editor at Paladin Press, for granting permission to use data excerpted from some of its publications.

Wolfe Publishing (Prescott, AZ) for granting permission to reprint quotes from Elmer Keith.

Mr. Andrew Branca, attorney-at-law and expert in self-defense law, for his book-publishing advice and permission to excerpt from his book.

Ms. Sarah Ann Zola, CreateSpace Editor, is especially appreciated and acknowledged for her comprehensive editorial review of my manuscript.

Most of all, I thank my wife Elizabeth Christian Traceski, my two dogs (Andy and Clutch), and my two cats (Buddy and Timmy) for providing love and family support.

About the Author

Frank T. Traceski is a retired rocket scientist and engineer who was a civil servant in the U.S. Department of Defense for thirty years. He held positions as a chemist; materials engineer; and missile, space, and launch vehicle engineer. He has a Bachelor of Science in chemistry (cum laude) from the University of Massachusetts (Amherst) and a Master of Forensic Sciences from the George Washington University. While at the U.S. Army Materials and Mechanics Research Center in Watertown, Massachusetts, he wrote military specifications for composite and transparent armor and a military standard for determining the ballistic resistance of armor. He is a member of the National Rifle Association and was a resident of Virginia for twenty years. He frequently used the NRA shooting range and visited the National Firearms Museum on many occasions.

www.ingramcontent.com/pod-product-compliance
Lightning Source LLC
Chambersburg PA
CBHW070231190526
45169CB00001B/152